WOMANSPIRIT

WOMANSPIRIT

A Guide to Women's Wisdom

HALLIE IGLEHART

1817

Harper & Row, Publishers, San Francisco

Cambridge, Hagerstown, New York, Philadelphia
London, Mexico City, Sáo Paulo, Sydney

Photographs on pages 38, 53, 62, 68, 113, 120, 136, 143, 159, and 176 are copyright © 1983 by Marcelina Martin.

The snake priestess sculpture pictured on page 38 is by Medea Maquis.

Dolls pictured on page 120 are by Mary Hope Whitehead Lee.

FIRST EDITION

Designer: Jim Mennick

Library of Congress Cataloging in Publication Data

Iglehart, Hallie.

WOMANSPIRIT: A GUIDE TO WOMEN'S WISDOM.

Bibliography: p.
1. Women—Religious life.   I. Title.
BL458.I37 1983   248.8'43   83-47724
ISBN 0-06-064089-8

88 89 90   10 9 8 7

Contents

Acknowledgments

Our lives are so interwoven that it is impossible to distinguish all the different strands from one another. In the same way, all the people who have influenced me and this book create a beautiful tapestry. I cannot separate you all out, although some of you will find yourselves represented on these pages. I thank you all—some for your encouragement throughout the years; others for your participation in Womanspirit groups, conferences, and rituals; still others for your simple and powerful presence.

Some of you have been directly, consistently, and invaluably helpful over the years. I'd like to thank Anne Armstrong for her psychic advice and commonsense, which has guided me through many major transitions. The information I received in a meditation led by Anne Barnett gave me the faith to persevere with the book despite several years of obstacles. And the healing hands and no-nonsense advice of the late Doris Breyer helped me through many years of growth. Romilly Grauer helped open doorways to wondrous places and lightened the way with her songs and humor.

A number of people have been instrumental in the production of the book. Neither the book nor I would be the same without the creative and often entertaining editing advice of Mary Jean Haley. Venetia Young patiently interpreted my many revisions in typing the manuscript. At a critical point, Vicki Noble read the manuscript and, on a psychic as well as a concrete level, offered essential help. John Loudon of Harper & Row has been a good-humored editor with many excellent ideas.

I am most grateful to four people. First, my parents, Harriet and Francis Iglehart, for their faith and support these past thirty-five years, and especially the last nine. I'd also like to thank Anne Kent Rush, who first suggested I teach Womanspirit, and who has always given generously of her advice and guidance over the years. Lastly, the vision, wisdom, and persistence of Marcelina Martin helped me finish the work.

Thank you all. This book is dedicated to you, and to all Womanspirits everywhere. May it help you as much as it has helped me.

Introduction

The Mother of Songs, the mother of our whole seed, bore us in the beginning. She is the mother of all races and the mother of all tribes. She is the mother of the thunder, the mother of the rivers, the mother of the trees and all kind of things. She is the mother of songs and dances. She is the mother of the stones. She is the mother of the dance paraphernalia and of all temples and the only mother we have. She is mother of animals, the only one, and the mother of the Milky Way. She is the mother of the rain, the only one we have. She alone is the mother of things, she alone.*

From the Kagaba,
a South American Indian culture

In cultures throughout the world, woman has long been recognized as the creation maker. She has been revered for her ability to give birth, to create food with her own body, to provide a large part (in many cases, most) of her people's food through gathering, and for her contributions to the spiritual and everyday life of the community.

The dominance of man as creation maker is a relatively recent phenomenon; yet today we have all been raised in a culture created almost exclusively by men, a culture that recognizes a male god as the creator of all physical life. And now some of man's creations, in particular his technology, offer him the role of the destruction maker, as we face the possibility of nuclear annihilation of the planet. We also face the possible destruction of our souls; for competitiveness

---

* As reprinted and edited by Judy Chicago for The Birth Project Exhibition, Unit 3, 1983.

and separation of mind from body, and human from nature, have caused an alienation of the psyche greater than any previously known.

We have become too imbalanced. It is time for women to rediscover and fulfill our roles as creation makers if this planet is to survive and women and men are to be able to live creative, harmonious, and truly productive lives. We must bring back the power of women's wisdom. This strength is not a power over anything else, but a force emanating from deep within each of us, radiating out into the world and connecting and interacting with others, creating a new definition of strength.

I believe that the synthesis of feminism and spirituality, called Womanspirit, is a major key to rediscovering this knowledge and power. Spirituality and politics are not separate, nor have they ever been. By examining our spiritual life we can see how it affects our material and everyday lives. Many of our images of who we are and of our power, or powerlessness, come from early spiritual and religious teaching. Even if we do not have a formal religious education, the values of established religions permeate all forms of education and media. Here are a few of these attitudes that we all grew up with: the creator is male; the body is separate from and inferior to the spirit; matters of the spirit need not affect those of politics; women are to follow men; power ultimately lies in someone else's hands.

I use the name Womanspirit to describe the path of the new creation makers for several reasons. I believe that the knowledge and wisdom evolving from women, individually and in groups, are essential to the healing and continued growth of our world. I have found that most meditations and spiritual practices taught by male-dominated religions and spiritual traditions are generally inappropriate for myself and other women. Certain approaches and techniques recur in women's spiritual groups, conferences, and rituals, and these seem particularly useful to women. All of the tools

I describe in this book were created by myself or are my adaptations of teachings by other women or cultures in which women have leading roles as creation makers.

> I am a woman giving birth to myself.
> We are women giving birth to ourselves.
> *Contemporary chant*

The development of our power comes from daily practices that strengthen our bodies, psyches, and souls. This book is written for women who want to learn techniques that they can use to become stronger and wiser in everyday life. By rediscovering our history as women myth-makers, artists, and healers, and by developing tools for creating new forms of consciousness through meditation, dreamwork, and ritual, we can recreate ourselves according to our own image. To develop a whole person, it is important to work on all parts of the self, and this can be done by approaching one's being through personal and collective history and mythology as well as inner meditation and dreamwork, natural healing as well as ritual. At some happy point, all the forms blend together and one learns to intuit and use whatever one needs. I use the female pronoun throughout the book, although these techniques may also be used by men who want to develop their more intuitive, gentle, deeper selves and better understand their own Womanspirits. In sum, the work is for all who want to learn from women's wisdom and rediscover the true nature of Womanspirit. Only by tapping our deep spiritual power and integrating it with action can we effect any lasting changes in our social, political, and economic condition.

I encourage you to work with others, as well as doing the exercises on your own. You can get together with a group of friends, organize a group and lead it yourself, or work with a roommate or partner. I have found the effect of the group energy in my classes and rituals to be far more powerful than any other spiritual teaching I have ever experi-

enced. Focusing on female energy in a group generates a
spiritual strength and sustenance that enable us to become
our own creation makers and to generate visions and practices for transforming the world around us. Since the group
energy is so important, and telling our stories is one of the
best ways for us to teach one another, I include many stories
from my own journey and those of my students. I have left
space in the book for you to record, in words or pictures,
your own responses to the exercises.

This book is made up of both basic and advanced techniques that may be used by individuals or groups.* It
follows the sequence I use in my classes, from history to
meditation, dreams to myth, healing to ritual. You need not
follow my sequence, however. Dip in and out of the book
according to your intuitions and needs. We are all the
creation makers, and a new world is awaiting creation. The
point is to follow your own path and discover your own
women's wisdom within the larger wisdom that we all share.

---

*Some of these exercises are included on *Womanspirit Meditation Tape*, by
Hallie Austen Iglehart, with original harp music by Georgia Kelly. For information on this tape, Womanspirit slideshow, reproductions (photos and
notecards) of images from this book, conferences, workshops, publications,
and other resources, send a self-addressed legal size envelope, with post-
age for two ounces, to: Women In Spiritual Education (W.I.S.E.), 1442A
Walnut Street, #313, Berkeley, CA 94709.

Chains of Fires

Each dawn, kneeling before my hearth,
Placing stick, crossing stick
On dry eucalyptus bark,
Now the larger boughs, the log
(With thanks to the tree for its life)
Touching the match, waiting for creeping flame,
I know myself linked by chains of fires
To every woman who has kept a hearth.

In the resinous smoke
I smell hut and castle and cave,
Mansion and hovel,
See in the shifting flame my mother
And grandmothers out over the world
Time through, back to the paleolithic
In rock shelters where flint struck first sparks
(Sparks aeons later alive on my hearth).
I see mothers, grandmothers back to beginnings,
Huddled beside holes in the earth
Of iglu, tipi, cabin,
Guarding the magic no other being has learned.
Awed, reverent, before the sacred fire
Sharing live coals with the tribe.

For no one owns or can own fire.
It lends itself.
Every hearth-keeper has known this.
Hearth-less, lighting one candle in the dark
We know it today.
        Fire lends itself.
Serving our life.
        Serving fire,
At Winter Solstice, kindling new life
With sparks of the old
From black coals of the old,
Seeing them glow again,
Shuddering with the mystery,
We know the terror of rebirth.

                                    ELSA GIDLOW*

---

*Moods of Eros (Mill Valley, California: Druid Heights Press, 1970), p. 20.
Used by permission.

1. The Discovery of Women's Wisdom

> There can be no doubt that in the very earliest ages of human history the magical force and wonder of the female was no less a marvel than the universe itself.
>
> JOSEPH CAMPBELL, *The Masks of God: Primitive Mythology*

My own discovery of my potential as a creation maker was a process of taking back control over my inner self, the root of my being, which I had previously surrendered to "experts" —who, as it happened, were almost all men and not of my own culture. This discovery and growing trust in my inner self has been one of the most joyful and sustained experiences I have known. As I go deeper into myself, I come in closer contact with the larger Self within me, the point of union with the life energy shared by all forms of life.

My Personal Journey

I grew up in the country on a farm. The changes of the seasons, the weather, the animals and insects and the trees, the moon and the sun were my teachers. I saw other children at school, and had four younger siblings, but I spent a lot of time by myself, and I often spent it reading. I consumed everything I could find about ancient cultures. I loved their mythologies, heroines, and goddesses. I read a book a day every summer, finding out about these powerful, vivid, goddess women. My other models were my mother and her mother, strong country women. Somewhere, far in the back of my mind, I had the idea that it was possible for women to have power and to express it directly. But the world told me otherwise, and I accepted this "reality."

From the time I was sixteen until I was twenty-one, I tried to find some answers to life in New Left politics. A lot of what I was doing made sense to me, but I was disturbed by the sexism and egotism of some male political organizers. At this time, however, I had never heard of sexism or power trips, and usually attributed my unarticulated questions to my own inadequacies.

As time went by, I focused my political work on my own more immediate needs. Over the years, I moved from work in civil rights, to poverty programs, to the antiwar movement, and finally to radical educational reform. At twenty-one, I followed this movement one step closer and started questioning my role as a woman; simultaneously, I was learning about yoga and meditation. I tried to find within myself and in eastern traditions some of the answers to changing the world that I was unable to find in the West and in politics. However, I found conflicts between my two new foci, as in this incident, recorded in my journal:

I love the smell of the incense and the music of the harmonium which fill the meditation room of this center. I am twenty-one. It is twilight, and I sit on the thick rug with the kindly plump swami and the three monks who live at the center. We sing in Sanskrit and meditate in silence for an hour. Even though I have never done anything like this before, I feel very peaceful and at home here.

But why is that man's photo on the altar with the flowers? I wonder. I thought he was just the founder of this organization and that he said there were no gods. . . . Maybe when I learn more I'll find out. . . .

The service is over and the youngest monk, Jana, who is new to the center, comes up to me. He towers over me in his orange robe and leans close.

"I was very impressed, Hallie, with how still you sat during the meditation. You obviously did this in other lifetimes and are already very progressed."

"Thank you, Jana."

"You know, I am having a hard time getting used to the rules of being a monk— celibacy is particularly hard for me, Hallie."

"That's too bad. I have to be going now."

Why do I have to deal with come-ons at a spiritual center? I feel angry at my vulnerability as the only young woman at the center.

But I am interested in Jana's ideas. As I walk home from the bus, I am fascinated by the possibility that I could have lived other lives. I feel overwhelmed; thoughts are whirling through my mind.

How can I be walking down the sidewalk right now, and also have existed in another time and place, perhaps many of them? And to think that I'm not really such a beginner, and that I won't have to struggle as much as I thought! . . . But do I really want to accept that status? Every system of reincarnation that I know of says that I have to be reborn as a man to make it spiritually. The men at the center, the swami and founder included, aren't any higher or better than I am. What do those words mean anyway— "higher" and "better?" . . . It looks like the same old hierarchy. Everywhere else it's a hierarchy of money and race. Here it's a hierarchy of consciousness. I became cynical about politics being able to change the world, but I thought that everyone would be equal in the spiritual world. But since I am not a man or "enlightened," I am supposedly inferior. . . . Now I realize what it feels like to be powerless, and I see that I really don't have much power in the material world, much less this particular spiritual one.

I am confused and angry. I decide once again that I'll have to look elsewhere for my answers.

For the next three years, I was torn, physically and psychically, between my feminist and spiritual selves. I worked in the feminist health movement in the United States, and traveled and studied spiritual practices in this country, Europe, and Asia.

At twenty-two, I traveled overland from England to Nepal and back. It was both exciting and frightening to be on the road, never knowing where we could camp next or what kind of people and land we would find. Twice we had to escape bandits. A dollar a day provided shelter, food, and transportation. I felt as though I had thrown myself wide open to the world.

In Turkey, I saw women veiled from head to foot. In the first town we came to in Iran, I had to walk down the streets surrounded by four western men for protection. Even so, Muslim men reached past them to grab at me. I was confused, angry, helpless, and outraged. I felt alienated and resentful towards my male friends, who, no matter how concerned they were about the sexism, didn't have to suffer through it as I did.

In India, my companion and I went to the mountains to escape the crippling heat. Later, having run out of money, I was hungry for most of each day and came to accept it. When I got sick, I felt the greatest physical pain I had ever known. I began to realize how protected I had been growing up in America.

I also found I had been deprived. For the first time since I was a child, I was able to experience the world's natural rhythms. During a cold winter in the Himalayas, on my second trip to Asia, I learned about the elements. The occasional sun meant warmth, light, safety, and a chance to wash. Night after night, I watched the cycles of the moon and stars. I learned that when the moon was new I could see her first white crescent in the western sky just after the sun had set. I felt what days and nights of extreme cold could do to a person. I learned about patience from depending on a fire for warmth, food, light, and tea. One freezing night, with snow two feet deep outside, my friend and I spent an hour trying to light the wet wood. Cold and hungry and not speaking to one another, we finally gave up. As we turned our backs, the fire suddenly flared up.

I learned as much from the Tibetans I lived near as I did from the mountains. I wrote in my journal:

It is a Himalayan March morning, still dark and cold. I am awakened by the sound of feet rushing in the street outside. I dress quickly in the clothes set aside for this day, making sure I have my white scarf with me to take to the temple.

It is the first morning of Losar, the Tibetan New Year, a celebration that lasts for a month. For weeks, hillfolk and nomads have been arriving in the marketplace, for this is the town where the Dalai Lama, who is the religious and secular leader, and the Tibetan government-in-exile are based. Every day new faces appear; new kinds of dress and dialects fill the street. Throughout the winter the remarkable chanting-singing voices of the members of the Drama School rang far up into the mountains as they practiced the six-hour-long folk operas they would perform as part of the celebration. We've all been waiting a long time for this morning.

My friends and I rush out onto the street. I feel incredibly excited and happy, as I did when I was a child at Christmas. Today, though, I feel community in a way I never did when I was younger. Dressed in their new clothes, everyone is coming out of their houses onto the street, greeting one another. We join the flow down the road to the temple. Hundreds of Tibetans, and a score of foreigners, are massed on the lawn of the courtyard. Most of the people I know from the market, the road, and mountain paths, the shops and restaurants. Now we are all gathered together for the first time. We smile, talk, use sign language, laugh.

We are surrounded by the sounds of the low drone of the monks' chanting; the blast of their six-foot-long trumpets, and the ringing of chimes and bells. The monks and the Dalai Lama have been performing rituals all night to welcome in the New Year. When the Dalai Lama appears on the balcony, we will go inside and throw our white scarves onto one of the three statues of the various manifestations of the Buddha and make a wish for the coming year. I think of Buddha as a wise person—not a god—but I respect the Tibetans' traditions and I have my scarf ready. I want my wish to be spontaneous.

The hours go by; everyone is waiting. The Dalai Lama is coming now! No—he isn't—later—Now! No! ... I look around at all the Tibetan faces and up to the mountains, which always seem to be protecting us. My eyes rest on the balcony. Suddenly, the Dalai

Lama materializes. I did not see him come out; he simply appeared. He grins at us, and I feel a rush of energy beaming from him to us and from us back to him. Love is a word I rarely use, but it is the only one I know to describe what is passing back and forth, surging around us.

In a crowd, we climb the twisting steps to the temple. Slowly, we edge our way forward. I have never felt anything like this before—the intense yet focused excitement, the beauty and power of the ritual and, most of all, the joy of the people welcoming a new cycle of the centuries. Once in the temple, I am part of the crowded flow moving towards the huge gold statues. I throw my scarf over my head; it catches on the upraised hand of the central Buddha. My wish soars with it! I feel whole—united with myself and with all the other people here. I've never known this feeling before. Is this the religious ecstasy that I've heard of—enlightenment, nirvana?

Living in a culture where the miraculous is part of everyday life radically changed my concept of reality. I had many experiences with the Tibetans that I might not have believed if they had not happened to me. One day during the New Year's celebrations, I watched a lama (priest) furiously blow his trumpet and wave his arms at the dark gray clouds that surrounded us for hundreds of miles. It was hailing so heavily that the morning's ceremonies might be ruined. The lama's trumpet rang louder, the ritual bonfire beside him burned higher. Moments before the scheduled start of the activities, a small patch of blue sky appeared directly above us. When the ceremonies were finished, the lama ended his ritual, the clouds closed over and the hail began again.

I learned from the Tibetans what it is like to live in a society where art, philosophy, and daily life are integrated with a religion that is sane and loving. I heard the word "compassion" used all around me, both in the most abstract teachings and by people on the streets. A Tibetan friend told me that I rarely saw Tibetan children crying or fighting because they were taught from childhood that all living creatures are part of the whole. Therefore fighting and violence are self-destructive. He told me how shocked the Tibetans were when they first came to India as refugees and saw people absentmindedly killing flies.

Tibetans constantly meditate with prayer beads, prayer flags, and prayer wheels so that all sentient beings might experience enlightenment. I love the Tibetans for their humor, wisdom, and rich culture. Their society reinforces wholeness, and the knowledge that this kind of integration can exist sustains me in my search.

Even in the peace of the Himalayas, however, I could not forget the first, unexpected, consciousness-raising experiences I'd had traveling overland to India. One incident in particular still stood out for me in its vividness and stark reality:

In Afghanistan, I decided one day to walk down the center of town without my usual male protectors, who ordinarily fended off the grasping hands of the Muslim men. As I headed towards the market, I felt a hand plunge into my crotch. Furious, I whirled around to hit the man. With horror, I realized that there were hundreds of black-robed men in every direction. If I let out my rage by confronting my assailant, it would be I who was killed. I retreated to my room.

As I tried to come to terms with the shock of this and many other such encounters, I realized, among other things, the power of religion. I knew that Muslim beliefs, which hold that women are of an inferior order than men, and which are reinforced daily by prayer, are intimately connected with the social and political status of women in Muslim countries. I saw that religions all over the world reflect and affect the role of women, usually in a destructive way. Christianity and Judaism generally teach that God is male and that women are to be meek—to say the least—and certainly cannot aspire to religious leadership. Even among the Tibetans there is sexism. In Buddhism, a woman must be reborn as a man before she can become enlightened, and relatively few women are allowed to enter the prestigious and influential religious life. In my spiritual quest, I found the hierarchy of consciousness of male-dominated religions to be as oppressive and self-serving as many political hierarchies. No wonder I couldn't find a religion or philosophy to nurture my emerging sense of myself as a worthwhile human being.

I realized that as a twentieth-century western woman, I could no longer look for answers outside myself and my culture. I wanted to find out whether other women shared my spiritual discoveries and perplexities. I hoped it was possible to uncover a women's spiritual consciousness as powerful as that which I had experienced with the Tibetans, but which was closer to my own inner being, and less oppressive.

Women's Spiritual Heritage

My traveling days over, I returned to the United States once again, found a job, and began to do volunteer work at the San Francisco Women's Health Center and the Women's Switchboard. I joined a consciousness-raising group and a women's studies program. The things I began to learn were more powerful than I expected.

Many of the experiences I had working in women's health care showed me that my "spiritual" self and my "political" self are not separate from one another. I had always hated the word "spiritual" because it implied that my meditations, my dreams, my creativity, and many other parts of my life were independent from the rest of myself. I realized that the division between my spiritual, political, and personal lives perpetuated my powerlessness. If I dismissed an intuition or meditation that related to my work, I denied my own wisdom and power. I felt this was a source that women were especially close to, whether biologically or sociologically. I was beginning to feel the connections between many of my parts. If the word "spirituality" meant anything to me, it meant integrating and acting from my whole self—my mind, my body, and my emotions—the union of personal and political, spiritual and material, inner and outer.

Although at the time, spirituality and holistic health were generally considered irrelevant and impractical in most feminist groups, I began to find others who were making discoveries and connections similar to my own. I wrote in my journal:

It is so simple. All I have to do is look inside myself, and to other women, and trust us and what I have intuited and known all along. We grow up thinking we didn't know anything—that our teachers and bosses and boyfriends and husbands knew better. But now I realize that we really do know—and that the world badly needs our ideas and our ways of being to regain its balance. I feel as though I have "come home."

I began reading about prepatriarchal history. At first, rather than accepting that women had indeed contributed many of the basic building blocks of civilization, I often doubted what I read or heard in classes, thinking that I simply "wanted to believe" in women's past power and authority. The roots of the fiction of male supremacy were deep in my soul. It took me a long time to dig them out and realize that women and women's work have in fact been overlooked and "written out" of history.

I read Elizabeth Gould Davis's *The First Sex* and Helen Diner's *Mothers and Amazons* and found that, contrary to what most conventional history books had taught us, women had a primary role in ancient culture.* They were honored as leaders, priestesses, healers, artists, inventors, and builders, as well as mothers, homemakers, and food providers. I learned that the biases that omitted women from history books had also labeled many cultures "primitive" when they were nothing of the sort. In fact, some early matrifocal cultures were egalitarian, communal,

---

*Elizabeth Gould Davis, *The First Sex* (Baltimore: Penguin Books, 1971); Helen Diner, *Mothers and Amazons* (Garden City, New York: Anchor Press/Doubleday, 1973).

peaceful, and, for their time, highly developed culturally and technologically.*

Much evidence indicates that these societies were far more peaceful, creative, and communal than ours, with few of the radical social and economic imbalances that predominate today's world. Cultures that find their main source of food by gathering, as did the majority of prepatriarchal cultures, are generally communal, with everyone helping run the community's affairs. Archeology shows us that there were no separate structures for rulers, for everyone lived and ruled together. The lack of fortifications and weapons in archaeological remains of such cultures as Catal Huyuk (Turkey, c. 3000 B.C.) and Crete (3000–1500 B.C.) indicates that both of these societies existed in peace for at least a thousand years. Significantly, there were altars and shrines everywhere, with no separate temples, indicating that spirituality was an integral part of everyday life. In *When God Was a Woman*, Merlin Stone makes the point that sexism, classism, racism, violence, and religious hierarchies came in with the patriarchy. For example, the concept of light being superior to dark (rather than being simply another part of the spectrum) was brought into India by the Aryans, the northern patriarchal invaders, to help assert their dominance over the peaceful, darker-skinned, goddess-worshipping Dravidian inhabitants.

Archaeological, anthropological, and historical evidence indicates that woman was the focus of human life and spirituality for millenia. This spirituality was the basis of a holistic worldview encompassing human relationships, material survival, and coexistence with all forms of life. Women's natural abilities to create life and food, plus their menstrual coordination with the cycles of the moon, were probably regarded as evidence of their intimate relationship with the

---

*See also: Merlin Stone, *When God Was a Woman* (New York: The Dial Press, 1976).

mysteries of the universe. Thus women were revered as shamans, healers, priestesses, and oracles.* (See Table 1.)

Learning about women's cultures has given me a new perspective on myself and my society, as well as inspiration for
making changes in both. My deep belief that the world need
not be and has not always been as sexist, racist, classist, and
violent as it is now has been confirmed. In fact, research
into other cultures made me realize that our society is even
more unbalanced than I had thought. An emphasis on
female energy is needed to restore the balance in the lives
and psyches of both women and men. Ignorance about
women and women's cultures perpetuates women's powerlessness and men's imbalance. Knowing about strong women
of the past has provided me with models and has helped me
believe in myself and in the potential of all women for
growth and survival. Meditating on these women and their
lives gives me a deeper understanding of my own potential.

These discoveries, and a desire to find other women with
whom I could explore spirituality, led me to teach my first
Womanspirit class. We focused on women's history, healing,
and meditation. As we sparked one another with our information and excitement, I felt my spiritual and political
worlds come together; we had tapped the power of a spirituality that affirms and strengthens women. As the past
decade has unfurled itself, Womanspirit has helped me discover unimagined strength within myself and learn how to
channel that power to help create peace in the world. I hope
that Womanspirit will help you as much as it has helped me.

Meditation: Women as Creation Makers

Your imagination is the basic tool you will use in Womanspirit meditations to help you achieve new freedom and
creativity and open long-closed doors. Developing an ability

---

*Anne Kent Rush, *Moon Moon* (New York and Berkeley: Moon Books/
Random House, 1976).

Cultures of Europe and the Mediterranean World

This chart provides a brief glance at some aspects of the prehistory and history of one part of the world. Scholars and scientists disagree somewhat on dates and interpretations of artifacts, which change with each new discovery, but the changes in women's status are widely acknowledged.

	PALEOLITHIC 35,000–8,000 B.C.	NEOLITHIC 8,000–3,000 B.C.	PRECLASSICAL 2,900–1,000 B.C.	CLASSICAL: GREECE AND ROME 1,000–100 B.C.	"DARK" AGES AND RENAISSANCE 100 B.C.–A.D. 1,600	MODERN INDUSTRIAL EUROPE AND UNITED STATES 1600–PRESENT
Livelihood	gathering and hunting	gathering and hunting, trade, agriculture, animal raising	agriculture, trade, fishing, animal raising	agriculture, fishing, trade, conquest by war	feudalism, trade, agriculture, rise of middle-class merchants	agriculture, trade, war, rise of industrialization and capitalism
Art	Cave Art (Europe): paintings and sculpture, lunar and seasonal calendars, breasts, vulvas, few human figures	Catal Huyuk (Anatolia, Turkey), 6,500–5,650 B.C.: statues of goddesses and female figures of youth, middle and old age, often with felines; paintings of ceremonies with death symbols	Minoan (Crete), 2,900–1,350 B.C.: bare-breasted priestess/goddess with snakes; pottery decorated with sea life; bull's horns (lunar) sculptures; women and animals predominate	realistic; human figures predominate; art idealized	mostly church dominates; later Renaissance: male artists predominate	male-dominated; increasingly abstract and technological
Status of Women	female figures predominate in art; women gatherers provide most of food in many places	female figures predominate in art; appearance of deities/goddesses	goddesses and priestesses predominate (as in Crete); matrilineal rulership (example: Egyptian dynasties); isolation of "female" powers	no vote; men dominant; a few women leaders in art and government; remnants of "Amazon" tribes led by women	a few women rulers and religious leaders; some women find more freedom in cloisters	technology frees women but devalues their work; women regain vote in the twentieth century, rise of feminism

Politics, Spirit, and Society	tribal, egalitarian, communal, technological; all aspects of life integrated; shallow caves and temporary structures used for daily life; deeper caves used for special ceremonies	Catal Hayuk: same platform structures used for meetings, working, ceremonies, sleeping, eating; dead buried directly beneath platforms; majority of burials are of women and children; integration of death and daily life	Minoan: "palaces" are used by all as living and working areas; peace for 1000 years; high level of technology	slave society specialized and stratified; previously holistic goddess divided into many weaker goddesses who are dominated by gods; warfare of city states and empires	stratified society; dominance of male god with female intercessor (Christianity); millions of women, men and children followers of nature religion, peasant revolutionaries and healers are burned as witches	religion separated from government and business; revival of "goddess" nature religions; women begin to regain some internal and external power in twentieth century; technology surpasses spiritual development

NOTE: Theories on the cause of the downfall of matrifocal cultures vary—Merlin Stone: invading patriarchal barbarians conquer peaceful matrifocal cultures; Jung: social and psychic need for balance of "masculine" element in matrifocal world; Sandra Roos: combination of above, with emphasis on rise of population and resulting specialization and technology, agriculture, private property, nuclear family, and division of labor.

to imagine a different way of living is a first step toward change. Visualization, or seeing an image in your mind's eye, is a common form of imagination. You may also imagine hearing, smelling, feeling, or tasting in a meditation. Or you may simply "know" intuitively what messages you are getting from your inner Self. All of these are valid ways of tapping your inner wisdom.

Try this meditation to imagine how different the world is when women are recognized as creation makers in all parts of life. Whenever I do it, it makes me feel proud to be a woman.

Take a few minutes when you can be quiet and undisturbed. Sit or lie down, making sure that you are comfortable, your clothes are not binding, and your breathing is unconstricted. When you are settled, take a few deep breaths to relax. Go over the events of the day in your mind. Then, begin to imagine what your daily life would be like from the time you got up in the morning, throughout the work of the day, until you went to bed at night, if you lived in a world where:

• your family name were passed down from mother to daughter

• the decision makers and organizers of your community were women

• the religious leaders of your community were women

• the women in your family and community were looked up to as the wise ones, the carriers of the most important knowledge, and the keepers of the mysteries of life

• when you are sick you went to the healing women for help

• when a special event came up, the women of your community gathered together to decide what to do

When you are finished imagining these situations, note what emotions, fantasies, and other reactions came up to you. You may want to express your responses in writing, drawing or dancing.

It is a well-known psychic axiom that if you begin to act as if something were true, it becomes more possible. Are there ways that you can begin to express the powers you felt in the meditation in your everyday life?

NOTES

Women's Art of the Past

I made some of my major discoveries about women's past and the power of art as a meditative source in a course taught by Sandra Roos, an instructor in art history and theory at the California College of Arts and Crafts in Oakland. She has gathered over a thousand slides of 32,000 years of art, including anonymous art that has been attributed to women. We cannot be sure who made what art in the past, but it is likely that a good deal of it was created by women. As Roos points out, the fact that women were important contributors to the cultural values as well as the art makes all of the art of the period especially significant. The class focused on the art of prehistorical Europe and Northern Africa, beginning with the Paleolithic period in about 30,000 B.C. Although Roos showed mostly art from Europe and Northern Africa, she pointed out that women's art of the past has been found in many parts of the world, including the Middle East, the Orient, and North and South America.

This art differs from our conception of art because it was a part of everyday life. The beautiful creations include many dwelling places, shrines, tools, ritual devices, textiles, ceramics, and calendars, as well as paintings and sculpture. Many people seemed to have participated in the artwork, and those who created it skillfully combined beauty with usefulness in a way not often seen in art today.

Much of the earliest prehistoric art has been found in caves. Caves are natural ways of being inside the earth, or the earth's womb, and some of the caves have natural vulva- and breast-like formations, often stained red or black, on the walls. Many of the notations found in the caves seem to refer to women's menstrual cycles and to other cycles of the year.* Perhaps these caves were used for rituals for psychic rebirth as well as for rituals involving physical birth.

Roos showed us a slide of the Paleolithic "Venus of Laussel," a large relief of a naked woman with one hand pointed to her belly and the other holding a crescent moon, which is carved above the entrance to a cave shrine. What would it be like, I wondered, to have such a sculpture above the door of a city hall or a church? I tried to imagine a society that placed as much emphasis on women and nature as did the societies of prehistoric times.

Seeing such art was a powerful meditation, one that completely reordered my sense of my own and other women's abilities, as well as the possibilities for all of human society. I let the images from the screen wash over me. When I closed my eyes, I could still see them, still feel their power—the staring eyes of the Minoan snake priestess, the black breasts and red vulvas of the cave walls, the bird-headed women with arms raised in a gesture at once commanding and blessing.

New emotions flooded through me—feelings of awe, strength, peace, grace, and an indescribable sense of power.

*Alexander Marschak, "Exploring the Mind of Ice Age Man," *National Geographic* magazine (January 1975).

Cretan Snake Goddess; Firenze, Museo Archeologico. This statue is one of many ancient representations of women and goddesses. Her wide eyes and the snakes wrapped around her imply the power of spiritual trance, while her strong stance and bare breasts reflect women's freedom. Photo: Alinari/Art Resource, Inc.

I tried imitating the expressions or poses of the images to find out, from the inside, what these women were like. I imagined myself as a woman sitting down with chisel or paint thousands of years ago to make the piece I was seeing. Leaping through time like this awed and excited me. It seemed almost incredible that human beings so long ago could have created art this close to my own private visions. Who were these women? What did they feel, think about? How were their lives different from ours; how the same?

As the class saw slide after slide of images of women, animals and plants, notations of lunar and seasonal cycles, and geometric figures, I knew I was seeing representations of the religion, economics, politics, and pyschology of thousands of years; and there was evidence to indicate that this art was made by women in societies in which women had a great deal of power. The early Paleolithic cultures maintained themselves by gathering and hunting. This made women, as the gatherers, important breadwinners, especially in those areas where gathering was the most reliable source of food. This undoubtedly gave women social importance as well, and it is most likely that women made some, if not all, of the cave art, as they stayed closer to the dwellings than the men, who went on extensive hunting trips. In addition, handprints, which are an important feature of some of the paintings, fit the hands of women's skeletons found nearby. Finally, the predominance of images of women, plants and animals, and lunar and seasonal notations confirm Roos's theory that "cave art," representing tens of thousands of years of human culture, could well have been made by women in cultures in which women had a central and influential position.

Roos pointed out that prehistoric cultures seem to have had a different relationship to divinity—the older female figures may simply be symbolic images and not goddesses, deification and externalization of divinity appearing as the society became more stratified. I loved imagining a woman making female images that are so beautiful that they are today generally referred to as goddesses, or objects of worship.

Much of the art indicates a sense of relationship with the rest of nature and the cosmos not common in western culture today. The predominance of plant and animal images indicates a reverence for nature and concern for understanding and working with other forces of life, rather than trying to control them. Power in these cultures seems not to have been one of "power over" or hierarchy, but a power emanating from within in creativity and wisdom, embracing the wholeness of life.

Roos describes this phenomenon in one of the more symbolic representations of woman's imagery:

Possible examples of holistic art from the Paleolithic period are the large number of what are sometimes identified as "vulva images"—circular images often slashed by a line. These were incised in rock as reliefs, or as aspects of stylized female figures.

These pieces can be interpreted on many levels simultaneously. As an image, the circle has obvious holistic implications, and this is why it has become a symbol of divinity. Identifying the slashed circle with female anatomy brings in a whole other world of associations that an abstract circle alone doesn't have. It's not only a continuous circular motif that implies infinity and encompasses everything, it also refers to woman, her vulva and her womb. The gut level association is with the source of life. The circle itself has always had those implications.

So there is this very complex image that embodies many levels of thinking and association and as such seems to be a perfect example of a holistic image. It doesn't isolate any one body of experience, but, by the image, encompasses a whole series of experiences, from the most finitely sexual to vast infinity. I think that female biology was used to express holism because of woman's ability not just to give birth but to give birth to her opposite, a male child. The female herself was bringing together various levels of existence in her very nature on a physical level—male and female. The female was at once the symbol of active power and the symbol of receptivity—qualities we now polarize as "masculine" or "feminine."*

When I left the class I sometimes saw women, incidents, or pictures that were clues that some of the energy that produced this art still persisted. When I saw strong women show delight in animals and a reverence for nature, I was reminded of the values of our foremothers.

As time went on, I began to recognize more and more the power of art to teach us about the past. The images come directly to us, unlike written history, which we receive secondhand or interpreted through the cultural filters that have written half of humanity out of history. We can respond to the images immediately—intellectually, emotionally, and physically. The beauty and strength of woman-oriented art from the past—and there is more to be discovered as research continues—has great implications for me about changing the present and creating visions for the future. I see and feel what life can be like for people when women have freedom and power, what we have been and what we can be. The revelations are so deep and startling that I sometimes physically feel a shifting inside my head or chest —the disintegration of centuries of self-doubt and conditioning. It is a continuing process.

Meditations

Living History

Works of art often contain messages that can only be understood if one *becomes* the work of art. This exercise will give you a context for the images you find in women's art of the past and will stimulate your own intuitive knowledge both of yourself and of women in other times and places. It will also help you transform powerless images of yourself into powerful images.

To begin: Take some time (half an hour to an hour) when

---

*Sandra Roos, personal communication, 1977.

you can be quiet and undisturbed. Immerse yourself in a visual source of art representing free women—you can use this book or one from the bibliography, a work of art, a museum exhibit, or a slide show. Have someone read these directions slowly to you or read them through yourself a couple of times to become familiar with the exercise. Make any adaptations you want.

• First, spend about five or ten minutes breathing deeply to relax yourself. Take full, deep, abdominal breaths. Allow your body to relax and your thoughts to become clear. Then allow your eyes to pass over, to caress the figures. Notice the postures, expressions, and any other details that seem significant. Feel your self—your body, your mind, your emotions— opening up to these images. Allow them to travel across the centuries to you. Feel your connection with the women who created these works. What were they thinking and feeling when they made them?

• Choose one image that particularly appeals to you. Immerse yourself in it. With your eyes closed or open, sit or stand the same way as the woman/goddess in the picture. How have you arranged your legs, chest, arms, neck? What expression do you have on your face? What are you wearing? How do you feel as this woman/goddess? What emotions arise? What thoughts?

• Imagine that you are the image talking. In the present tense, describe out loud what you are experiencing. Who are you? Where do you come from? How do you feel, move, and think? Do you have anything to say to your everyday self?

• What are you experiencing that relates to the rest of your life? Know that this image is a part of you and that you can come back and communicate with her whenever you want.

• When you are ready to end the meditation, thank the woman-image and the woman who made it for communicating with you. To help bring yourself back, notice your breathing—where it is and how it moves. Become aware of your feet, calves, thighs, pelvis, belly, back, chest, arms, hands, neck, and head. Touch the different parts of your body. Massage them if you want. If your eyes are still closed, slowly open them and notice how the world looks with your new eyes. How do you feel? Are you and the world different than you were before the meditation?

If you want to record your responses or anything inspired by them in writing, drawing, or other art forms, do so. You may want to live out the experience in the rest of your life by your attitudes and actions. Whatever you do, remember that the energy that you experience comes from within you and through you and that you are the source and channel of this strength.

NOTES

I chose the statue of the first century Roman goddess Luna on page 59 of Rush's *Moon, Moon* for my meditation. Here's my response:

With my eyes closed, I stand on tiptoe, my arms open and slightly raised, my head gently leaning forward. My robes are blowing in the wind and my cloak hovers behind me like wings. When I feel the cloak, my shoulder blades relax on either side of my spine. I have a crescent moon on my head and this makes me stand taller, my neck and spine easy. I feel light yet very strong. I imagine that I am flying through the air looking down at the earth.

I talk to the earth. "Earth, here I am again with my crescent moon. I am continually waxing and waning in your sky. The cycles of your seasons move more slowly than my phases. Sometimes you feel heavy. I bring you lightness and change."

I open my eyes and start to move around the room with light steps, my arms outstretched. I feel that I have a lot of strength to use in dealing with the city outside my window.

"Earth," I say, looking at the trees, "I bring you moisture and light for your growth. I bring you the promise of continued renewal. Every month I come to you and am born, grow, decrease, and die. And then I am born again. You and I have been dancing this dance for millions of years and will do so for millions more."

I feel comforted by this broad view of time. As I move, I see in the next room my desk and table with all my bills and business papers. I experience a tremor of the anxiety I often have in deep meditation when I am confronted with difficult business matters. I move around the room some more, trying to shake off the feeling. It won't leave me, so I ask Luna-Hallie for help. She says, "Hallie, you needn't be afraid that you won't be able to deal with business matters. You needn't be afraid that you will become lost in the consciousness that you are in now. You won't die to the rest of the world. You are always changing, just as I am. And just as I am always reborn and come back, so do you. Sometimes I am a crescent; sometimes I am full. Sometimes you are meditating; sometimes you are working out the material necessities of your life. Your constant change keeps you alive. Your cells die and are reborn every second. When you have finished this meditation, you will allow that experience to end, to 'die.' And you will be reborn to the next—hassling over money. Your body and your mind will remember and be nourished by the strength and wisdom you feel now. Within the death of each experience is the seed for the next. Your other parts and papers will always be waiting for you! Don't be afraid, Hallie. You will not die."

Now I feel more in control of my life. I can walk through it more easily than I could before. I know that I can trust myself to move more lightly and yet still be in touch with the earth. I thank Luna for reminding me about my own cycles and my own continu-

Luna, Roman, first century A.D.

ing strength. I thank myself for facing my fear of being lost in an inner space.

I take several deep sighs and feel my breath moving my chest. My jaw loosens. I see the birds flying outside. I bring myself back to my body—first mentally, by noticing different parts, then physically, by rubbing myself all over. The sensation of my ankle bones is especially strong as I rotate my feet. I notice much more around me; everything looks closer and more vivid than it did before. I am aware of my belly and chest and feel solidly on the earth.

I am peaceful. I go back to work.

Group Meditation: A Birth Ritual

Doing meditation in a group is an extremely powerful way to tap into personal and collective consciousness. Try this alone or in a group. Share your meditations afterwards.

Spend a few minutes relaxing yourself. Have someone read these directions to you or read them yourself, pausing at various intervals to close your eyes and feel, see, hear, or otherwise sense and imagine what it would be like to be a woman taking part in a ritual such as this one, which might have occurred in prehistoric caves.

Imagine:

• It is time for you to go through your first rebirth ritual. Perhaps you have just started menstruating, or had an important vision or dream or gone through some kind of crisis. You will acknowledge the changes in your life through the ritual. Imagine that you have fasted for several days before the ritual, and your family and friends care for you, and the wise woman of your tribe advises you in your preparation. The day finally comes.

• Imagine that everyone gathers together her special objects of power. You are particularly careful in your choice. You want to carry only one thing with you into the cave that you can keep as a physical reminder of your rebirth. Using red clay and white powder, you all paint yourselves. Your mother draws on your back the sign she chose for you at your first birth.

• Imagine that as you make your way to the cave, you all

chant and sing in low tones and wave branches to dispel unwanted energy and to draw in the spirits of your new birth.
When you reach the entrance to the cave, you must crouch
down low, perhaps crawling in darkness on your knees a long
distance. The earth and gravel under you reminds you of your
original mother—the earth. Finally you reach the cave itself.
It is large, but torches light up all of it. The ground is hard,
trampled by many feet during other rebirth rituals. The torch-
light flickers on the red painted breasts that have been
smoothed out of the walls. You have been here many times
before for other people's rebirths. Now everything looks larger and more vivid. Your senses are heightened by your fasting
and your days of meditating on the changes in your life.
Helped by friends, you climb into the womb —a long crevice
in the wall that has been smoothed out and painted red.

• Experience your family and friends standing in a semicir-
cle facing you, humming a long deep sound and swaying
slowly back and forth. You curl up into a fetal position, feeling
the dark warmth of the earth all around you. You begin to
remember what it was like before the changes happened in
your life. You love that self, but now, as you hear the humming
growing louder, you feel how much you welcome your new
self, how much you want to be reborn. You start to uncurl,
slowly feeling each muscle as though for the first time. Twisting and writhing you begin to undulate in the womb. The
chanting is growing louder now. Feeling every possible movement, you begin to slip smoothly down the crevice. The moment before your head reaches the lip, you hestitate—and
then thrust yourself out into the new world to be caught by the
open hands of your kin. They are singing high and clear now,
stroke you, smiling down at you, and carry you over to the
rounded breasts of the cave. Many hands lift you up to the
breasts and you feel all the richness of the earth pouring out
to you. As you feel the love and rejoicing around you, you
know that your new life is welcome and will be as nourished
and as rich as was the old.

• When you are ready to come out of the meditation, stretch your body and touch yourself all over. Slowly open your eyes and look around the room. Write, draw, dance, or tell your meditation experience. Remind yourself that you can carry the insights and strength you gained in the meditation into your everyday life.

NOTES

ART BIBLIOGRAPHY*

Gimbutas, Marijas. *Goddesses and Gods of Old Europe, 6500–3500 B.C.: Myths and Cult Images.* London and Berkeley: Thames & Hudson and University of California Press, 1974.

Hawkes, Jacquetta. *Dawn of the Gods.* New York: Random House, 1968.

Lhote, Henri. *The Search for the Tassili Frescoes.* New York: Humanities, 1973.

Lippard, Lucy. *Overlay: Contemporary Art and Art of Prehistory.* New York: Pantheon Press, 1983.

Matz, Friedrich. *The Art of Crete and Early Greece.* New York: Crown, 1962.

*The text accompanying these pictures is sometimes marred by sexist interpretations of the art.

Mellaart, James. *Earliest Civilizations of the Near East.* New York: McGraw-Hill, 1965.

National Geographic magazine. "Spectacular Treasures from a Chinese Tomb" (May 1974); "Drought Threatens the Tuareg World" (April 1974); "Exploring the Mind of Ice Age Man" (January 1975).

Neumann, Erich. *The Great Mother.* Princeton, New Jersey: Princeton University Press, 1963.

Noble, Vicki. *Motherpeace.* San Francisco: Harper & Row, 1983. (See also Motherpeace Tarot Deck, by Karen Vogel and Vicki Noble, published by Motherpeace, P.O. Box 1511, Cave Creek, AZ 85331.)

Piggott, Stuart. *Ancient Europe.* Chicago: Aldine, 1965.

Rush, Anne Kent. *Moon, Moon.* New York and Berkeley: Random House/Moon Books, 1976.

Sjöö, Monica, and Mor, Barbara. *The Great Cosmic Mother.* Trondheim, Norway: Rainbow Press, 1981.

WomanSpirit magazine. 2000 King Mt. Trail, Wolf Creek, Oregon 97497 (back issues available).

Womanspirit Photomythology Reproductions. Notecards and photographs by Marcelina Martin, including photographs from this book. For brochure and article on Photomythology, send SASE to: W.I.S.E., 1442A Walnut Street #313, Berkeley, CA 94707.

Other books and materials may be useful as background material on prepatriarchal history and other aspects of Womanspirit. Try libraries, feminist bookstores, spiritual bookstores, and special sections of general bookstores. You can also obtain bibliographies, according to subject matter, from A Woman's Place Bookstore, 4015 Broadway, Oakland, CA 94611. Yes! Inc., 1035 31st St., N.W., Washington, D.C. 20007 publishes two catalogs, *Inner Development* and *Wellness,* which have extensive listings of books in these areas. Womanspirit Catalog, 1442A Walnut Street #184, Berkeley, CA 94707, carries books, tapes, notecards, jewelry and art.

2. Tapping Inner Guidance Through Meditation

I found God in myself and I loved her fiercely.

NTOZAKE SHANGE,
*For Colored Girls Who Have Considered Suicide
When the Rainbow Is Enuf*

Once we have replaced our negative images of ourselves with positive ones, we can begin to tap even greater depths of our inner wisdom. Meditation is a process of going back into the void, the womb of our consciousness, to rest, regenerate and create anew. We go deep inside ourselves, find new ideas, information, and images, and apply them in our daily lives. Thus we become more self-directed; for, as we discover the accuracy and effectiveness of our women's wisdom, we learn to trust our spontaneity and our judgment. Meditating on a regular basis was one of the major forces in changing me from a determined, daring girl who didn't know what to do with herself to a woman who now can direct and create her own life and who knows how infinite are her inner resources—and, most importantly, how to use them.

The meditations in this book are specifically designed to tap women's inner wisdom and translate it into practical and creative action. Much of what we know—both intuitively and rationally—is layered over by decades of learning to doubt ourselves and giving over much of our decision-making and creation-making power to others. By meditating, we can go past these layers of conditioned self-doubt and discover our own wisdom. This wisdom may come from our bodies' knowledge of the nature of giving birth and of cycles, or it may come from previously suppressed intellectual and artistic creativity.

I describe meditation as a focused state in which all aspects of one's consciousness are integrated. If a person is engrossed in a math problem, for instance, and if all of her attention is on it—if her emotions are directed toward it through her excitement and interest, her intellect is fixed on it, and her body is relaxed and her breathing free—then she is meditating on the math problem. Depending on a person's qualities of attention, she can also be in a meditative state when she is exercising, working, drifting into reverie, or involved in any other activity. Meditation is more ordinary and accessible than most people realize. It seems mysterious and out of reach because it is not traditional in the West; but all of us enter meditative states, whether or not we recognize them.

Women and Meditation

Because women are brought up to be introspective, intuitive, quiet, and receptive, we usually find traditional meditation easier than men do. Most meditation practices were developed by men for men, and most women, and some men, at this point in history, have different needs. In fact, most meditations that evolved within a patriarchal framework are unsuited for and often destructive of women.

In this culture, men are generally raised to be rational, unempathetic, and aggressive, and the meditations designed for them are intended to help them learn to be more receptive and sensitive. Historically, these meditations have come from hierarchical religions and cultures and have been rigidly prescribed, hierarchically transmitted, other-worldly, and ascetic. Often focusing on withdrawal from the world, they emphasize quieting and controlling the mind and body. In certain disciplines, this involves suppressing these parts of ourselves for some "higher" ideal.

Women are too used to being quiet and controlled, and for us there is a fine line between quieting ourselves and suppressing ourselves. We have been withdrawn from the world outside our homes for too long. We have made some political advances in the last hundred years, but each of us still carries the internal attitudes that result from living in an unbalanced society. The healthy cycles of our bodies have been regarded as unclean aberrations.

We want to enliven and enjoy our bodies, our rational and intuitive minds, and our emotions. We want to free our energies to act in the world, not suppress them. As a result, we need meditations that are designed for women. We need meditations that help us be active, love ourselves, and develop and use the full power of our inner strength in our personal and public lives.

The evolution I have gone through in ten years of developing Womanspirit meditation techniques reflects a discovery of women's unique needs, strengths, and collective psychic power. Learning to trust my own judgment and intuition about what forms of meditation, if any, to use has been as important as meditating itself.

Having focused successively on several different kinds of meditation, I now use different tools whenever they are appropriate. Each has been suitable at different times for different reasons, and I have interwoven all of them. Some forms of meditation I needed to do because I needed an outside structure, others because I needed to develop my inner self, still others because I wanted to integrate my inner being more with my outer self.

Meditation Diary

This diary of my years of meditation, beginning in 1969, reflects an evolution similar to that of many women I know and points out the need for flexibility and diversity, as well as dedication. I have learned to make a Womanspirit approach toward meditation and spirituality—an approach that recognizes individual differences and needs, and which is based on trust in oneself as teacher, guru, guide.

Year 1: Traditional Hindu meditation of visualization, chanting, and breathing. Good for structure and discipline. Understand intellectually the reasons for doing it but feel something is missing.

Year 2: Zen Buddhism seems the deepest wisdom. I make attempts at zazen—sitting and counting my breaths. Most of the time I hate it, feel like a failure, but keep trying, since I don't know what else to do, and since the idea of enlightenment is very mystifying and appealing. I finally recognize that zazen is too exclusively mind-oriented for me. I need to experience my body and emotions more. Have an enlightenment-like experience doing karate.

Years 3 to 5: Doing Jungian inner guide meditation [see this chapter]. I like this meditation because it is more active, creative, and practical. I learn a lot about pacing myself: to practice meditation regularly, but to recognize when it's gone on too long, so that I don't get spaced out. Inspired by guide meditation, I start doing artwork for the first time in ten years. I find that doing bodywork on someone or having it done on me is one of the deepest meditations I have ever experienced.

Year 6: Dreamwork, mostly the Malaysian Senoi method [see Chapter 3]. Seems more of a direct link between my inner life and my outer life, and I can see changes in both. At first, I have problems letting go of guidework and recognizing the importance of dreamwork. Also discover walking and sitting under trees as meditation—solutions become obvious, mind calms. Do frequent group meditations. Decide that enlightenment is a gradual process, not the sudden awakening I'd hope for.

Years 7 to 10: Start waking up and wanting to start day immediately, not taking time to write down or work with dreams. Worry about this for a while, until psychic teacher confirms my feelings and suggests meditation consisting of occasional sitting and inviting as much energy as I can handle to flow through me. Resolve to trust my own intuitions more and not have to wait for outside approval. Sit for a few minutes in morning and night, say a few words, ring my chimes, and let the words and feelings move through me with the sounds. Forgotten ideas and images of the day float up. Do many little meditations throughout the day and start to allow these to become more spontaneous, doing them or making them up when I need them— or not doing any. Doing rituals alone and in a group becomes a powerful focusing tool [see Chapter 6].

Usually stop at different times throughout the day and cover my eyes with my hands to relax my eyes. Writing becomes a meditation, as I re-experience, in a deeper way, knowledge and experiences from my life of the last few years. Realize that I have become a lot clearer and more focused, so that I am "meditating" in everyday parts of my life. Discover the joys and peace of harmonious physical movement in swimming and dancing.

Year 11: Not meditating formally as much, but spend more time quietly listening to music. Have my "Good Earth Experience": one day, sitting in a very ordinary restaurant, I have spontaneous enlightenment experience—an extreme change in consciousness—far greater than any I've ever had before. It lasts for many hours. I see light radiating from everything—from machines and concrete as well as from trees and grass. Everything seems exquisitely beautiful and more than three-dimensional. When I look into people's eyes it's as though I can look deep into their souls. My mind is almost completely silent, and when I do hear it, it is like a far-away voice trying to get my attention. I feel total love and acceptance for all I see, yet I can still discriminate between suffering and nonsuffering. In fact, I realize that because I am not resisting any part of my world, I have far more energy than ever before. In this highly "spiritual" state, I am even more capable than ever of making "political" change.

Years 12 to 14: I learn to stimulate mini-versions of my "Good Earth Experience" with certain music, light, circumstances. Use formal meditations as needed, though I "need" them less than before. Focus on bringing more awareness into my physical body.

My inner and outer lives have become more integrated. At first they were entirely separate; with guidework they were more related; then bodywork and dreamwork continued the synthesis; and now I finally feel as though I am a whole person, using whatever meditation is necessary whenever I need it. More and more, I am able to act, feel, and think from that centered wholeness I have developed through meditation, so that I need a formal meditation less and less.

All the meditations I did were a way of going deep inside myself, past the busy surface chatter of my rational mind. With the more active meditations, I could use the resources of that inner self to work with questions, problems, and creative projects. My meditations supplied some of my best ideas for writing, teaching, and ritual. I was astounded at the richness of my inner self, from which I had been cut off by years of exclusive emphasis on rational thinking.

I have come full circle—for the point of zazen, one of the first forms of meditation I tried and rejected for its rigidity, is not to be sitting, but to develop a constant awareness in everyday life, in which everything becomes a meditation. To do this, I had to create my own Womanspirit path, forge my own journey from a traditional, passive, structured, intellectual, eastern, traditionally male meditation; to the still very structured but more androgynous western, active, intuitive guidework; to the more traditionally female earthy, "primitive," active dreamwork, group meditations, and bodywork; and finally, to my own meditation—spontaneously using and creating whatever tools I need. I feel fewer and fewer divisions between "female" or "male," structured or loose, eastern or western, and my life has a strength that comes from knowledge of my inner self.

• Are there some activities you do that you never recognized as meditation? If you meditate formally, note what works for you and what doesn't. If you are just beginning to meditate, describe why you want to meditate. Use words, images, sounds, movement, and so on.

NOTES

Meditation Guidelines

Most meditation practices start off by directing attention inward. In this chapter, I refer alternately to "meditating" and "going inside." Later chapters discuss more active meditations. Our inner selves have been neglected, denied, or distrusted, and meditation is an essential tool in reclaiming lost inner territory. However, this does not mean that we should withdraw and focus only on our inner selves. Being responsible in outer-directed activities is an important part of realizing personal power and is helped by work inside. When we discover the still, quiet place that lies within each of us, we can see it as a base to untangle ourselves from the doubt, indecision, ill health, guilt, and other forms of old programming that result in confused and diffused actions.

Doing any kind of inner meditation can be relatively easy or quite difficult, depending on your personality, your mood, your preparation, and the situation. Don't be discouraged if you feel blocked at first. A common complaint is: "I keep thinking about other things." Notice a distracting thought, tell yourself you will come back to it later with a much clearer mind—and let go of it.

A second problem can come from thinking that meditation is a special state, and being afraid that you are not meditating if you feel like you are daydreaming, dozing, or being creative. All of these states are forms of meditation, and there are probably many more that we experience in our lives but don't recognize. With practice, it becomes easier to recognize the varying states of meditation and to focus oneself. In doing meditations such as the inner guidework I describe here, some people say, "I feel like I'm just making this all up." Of course you're just making it all up! It's all coming from you, and that's the point of these meditations —to tap your inner self. It is a step towards realizing that our inner selves are part of us, not something that comes from the outside.

People also sometimes worry that they aren't doing a meditation like inner guidework "right" because they can't "see" anything. Many people do not receive their inner information visually. Some hear words or phrases, others simply "know" the answer. You will discover your own way of perceiving your inner life. Since most of us are used to perceiving our world by sight and sound, being able to see and hear inside ourselves usually helps make the meditation more real for us. Try to develop other senses as well, allowing images, sounds, smells, textures, tastes, ideas, memories, or emotions to emerge.

The point of meditation is to open your creativity and self-directedness. Learning specific methods is like getting a map to a territory new to you. Once you have learned your way, you don't need the map until you start to explore yet another new region. Try doing meditations as suggested here, and be open to any changes or additions you'd like to make. Trust your developing intuition, wisdom, and spontaneity. Singing, dancing, making symbolic objects or movements often best express the depths reached in meditation. Create your own version of these meditations—ones that suit you, the time and place, and the people you may be with.

How to Make a Meditation Space

It is a good idea to set aside a special place and time to meditate, especially when you are beginning to practice. Every house in India, no matter how crowded, has a corner of a room where a person can sit undisturbed. You can make your own place to meditate, be quiet, center yourself, do bodywork and other healing work. As you use this space more and more, you will find that as soon as you are there, you will feel peaceful and centered.

I created my first meditation space in my bedroom simply

by setting up a floral-patterned 1930s bench with an African violet plant and my Tibetan chimes placed on it. Every night before I went to sleep I would sit and meditate briefly. I now have several meditation sites, one on the hearth of a bricked-up fireplace, and another in a shallow closet that I lined with old lace curtains and velvet. As soon as I sit or stand at these places, I feel centered and peaceful and am able to focus my thoughts.

To make a meditation space, decide where in your house or outdoors you would like to place it. You can walk around and sit in different places to discover which feels the best to you. Pay attention to the difference in the direction you are facing, the quality of the light, whether you face a wall or window, and whether there are any distractions.

You can make meditation spaces in many places, each for a different purpose: one for meditating, a kitchen or dining room table for food meditation, a creative space with art materials, a household altar near your front door. Balinese women make new offerings daily and carry flowers, food, and incense to create altars throughout their environment.

To make a meditation table, you can use a favorite table you already have, or you can build one. Choose materials for their textures and meaning for you. You can make a simple, inexpensive, beautiful altar from boards and bricks. You can add something from each of the four elements, and your own special objects:

• Earth: Put something living—a favorite plant, herbs, or fresh flowers — on your table.

• Air: Incense wafting through the air can change your mood and fill the whole house with a ritual atmosphere. You can get many different kinds of stick incense. A good stick incense holder is the kind used in Asia: Fill a bowl with rice, barley, sand, or other natural material. When you light the incense, stick it in the bowl—it will stay upright and the ashes will mingle with the grains. A powerful Native American tradition involves burning sage in a bowl, inhaling a little of the smoke, and blowing or waving the smoke over different parts of your body, thus smoking yourself as a psychic cleansing.

• Fire: Candles bring life and help you focus. Choose candles for their colors and textures. Beeswax candles smell and feel wonderful and drip into beautiful shapes. Other candles come in a larger variety of colors and drip less. When using candles, make sure they are secure and that you extinguish them when you leave the room or if you begin to fall asleep.

• Water: Keep a seashell, starfish, or bowl of clear water on your table to invoke the ocean.

• Sound: Use bells, Tibetan chimes, flute, Japanese bowls, music box, or other music-making tool—you can make a simple one by tying jingle bells onto a ribbon or stick.

• Your own ritual objects: Choose a favorite picture, crystal, photograph, hanging, or other object that has special significance for you. As you use them in rituals, their power to inspire you will increase.

When you meditate, be sure to wear loose, comfortable clothing of natural materials so that you can breathe easily and allow your electromagnetic (as in acupuncture) energy to flow freely.

To initiate your meditation space, find a way to sit or lie in your special place so that your spine is straight and you are comfortable. You can use a mat or rug, pillow or chair. Take a few deep breaths. Look at everything you have gathered together. Light the candles and some incense and hold one of your special objects in your hands. State your purpose in building this meditation place—your hopes, needs, how you will use it in your daily life. Know that as your life unfolds you will have all that you want—and more. Sing, chant, or play your instrument. When you are finished, thank the space and material objects, extinguish any fire and rest quietly for a moment.

Basic Relaxing Meditation

This is an important basic exercise in and of itself. In addition, it, or your adaptation of it, should be done as an introduction to all the exercises in this book.

If you try to come in from work and immediately sit down to meditate, chances are that your mind will still be busy with the energy of the place, people, or activity you have just come from. One of the reasons modern life is so tiring is that our attention is usually scattered throughout the day over several places—home, office, where we run errands, a friend's house—and over time—what we just did, what we have to do next. It is very renewing to reduce the amount of exposure and stimulus to pull the attention back into the center of the self.

Taking five, ten, or thirty minutes to allow yourself to quiet down physically, emotionally, and mentally can make an enormous difference in your energy, peace of mind, and clarity of thought. Releasing and centering your energy is a meditation itself, as well as a way of focusing yourself before and after other types of meditation.

Coming out of meditation too quickly can be very jarring and disorienting and can detract from the meditation. Centering your energy at the end of a meditation will prevent the sometimes uncomfortable feeling of being too "spacey." The more often you do this meditation, the easier it will become for you to become centered, so that you can do it in a few minutes.

To begin:

Find some time and space when you can be quiet and undisturbed. This is easier if you are alone and in a place that is comfortable, but you can be anywhere— on the bus, in the bathroom, at work, waiting for someone, or lying on your bed. Have someone read these directions to you or read them into tape recorder and play it back to yourself or your group. Allow enough time after each sentence to follow the meditation. If you wear glasses or contact lenses, remove them before you start to center yourself.

Lie or sit comfortably with your arms and legs uncrossed and your spine free. Loosen any clothing that feels restrictive, such as tight pants or shoes. You want to be able to breathe fully. Take a minute to feel how you are sitting or lying. Which parts of you feel open? Which are tight? Are there some parts that feel as though they are more pulled from the floor or chair than others? Take one deep breath so that you can feel your belly, diaphragm, and chest expand, and gently let the air out through your mouth. Exhaling through the mouth helps your jaw—a major tension area—be loose. Any time you want to change position to accommodate the releases in your body, do so. Tell yourself that you are letting go of any tensions, pains, or anxieties for these moments.

Continue inhaling through your nose and exhaling out your mouth, but don't force your breath. Simply let it come and go in its own natural rhythm and fullness. Allow yourself to breathe in this way for a minute or two. Next, imagine that when you inhale you send your breath to a part of yourself that you would like to feel more open. It may be the lower back, the shoulders, the head, or some other part. Feel your breath caressing that part. When you exhale, feel your breath carrying away any mental or physical tensions that you want to leave you. Know that you can let go of them for now—you don't need them. When you inhale, tense slightly the part of your body that you want to release. When you exhale, gently release it. Do this for about five minutes. Observe any images, emotions, or thoughts that arise and then let them also pass by. Do another part, if you want.

When you are ready to stop, bring your attention back to all the parts of your body. How are you sitting or lying? Do you feel different than you did when you began? Touch yourself all over. Slowly open your eyes. With your new eyes and body, spend a few minutes looking and moving around.

Daily Meditations

Every morning and/or evening, sit at your meditation space. Do the basic relaxing meditation described above. You may also do any of the following:
• Paint or draw, symbolically or literally, how you are feeling about yourself, your life, or a particular issue. You may draw spontaneously, letting the figure communicate to you. Pay attention to the dynamics and colors. Now draw another picture to represent any changes you would like to make in this area. What does your picture show you? How can you act on this message?
• Light a candle and incense and, as they burn, concentrate on a particular quality or attitude you want to bring into your

life, such as peace, assertiveness, or focus. Whenever your mind wanders, gently bring it back. Meditate on your chosen topic until you feel complete.

• Make a list of everything that is going on in your life. Go through each area and congratulate yourself for it; "Congratulations for confronting that difficult situation!" "Congratulations for getting those plants repotted for the first time in two years!" "Good for you for creating work and relationships that are good for you now."

• Make a list of parts of your life you would like to change or are working on. Then put these statements in the form of an active sentence: "Right now, I am learning more and more about making my work more beneficial for others and more productive for myself." Feel the truth of this reality strengthening your body, your thoughts and your emotions.

NOTES

Working with an Inner Guide

An inner guide is the "imaginary" personification of the wisest, most centered part of ourselves. Since we are used to relating to the human form, and most of what we meditate on is human activities, imagining a guide in human form usually makes communication easier and less threatening. In the directions, I refer to a female guide, although a guide can be female, male, or androgynous. In one sense, lovers, teachers, friends, people we admire or respect—living and dead—are all our guides and we their guides. However, since an inner guide is the personification of your own unique knowledge, she is not someone you know in ordinary life. This helps avoid projecting too large a burden on another person.

You can have different guides at different times in your life, but it is generally a good idea to focus on one at a time. This way, you can build up your relationship with a particular part of yourself, rather than dividing your attention. You will find many other figures inside to help you deal with the various aspects of your life: one figure for your work life, one for your relationships, one for your political life, one for your transportation, one for your sense of play, one for your pets, and so on. The figure who helps guide you in your interaction with all of these is your inner guide.

Working with an inner guide is one of the most powerful, effective, and affirming meditations I know. All the strength and wisdom that I need is inside me, but it gets scattered and obscured by my lack of faith in myself and by the absence of outside confirmation. Contacting my inner guide is an immediate experience of my own strength, resourcefulness, and creativity, and it is especially important as I change my self-limiting conditioning as a woman. I become more my own authority, and learn to rely on myself and my intuition. Contacting my guide also helps me center myself, resolve problems, make decisions, get more perspective on my life, and acquire information. It is an important reference point for doing any kind of psychic or inner work, because my guide will always set me straight if I get off balance.

Doing inner guide meditation was my first exploration of my internal reality: my symbols, archetypes (figures representing a part of one's psyche that is often universal—i.e., the wise old woman), dynamics, landscapes, and the like. This technique was structured enough so that I could trust it and follow it into my depths—where I discovered amazing parts of myself that I never knew existed. The changes in me were manifested by increased confidence, creativity, and artistic ability, as well as making me more practical and decisive.

Sometimes the guidework was my avenue to psychic healing. For instance, I might be conflicting with someone I knew. If I meditated and dialogued with my inner guide and with my inner image of the person, I would always come to a better understanding of the situation and feel more peace and forgiveness. Often I would see the person later and find that her attitude had also "magically" changed. Sometimes she would give me a gift just like the one I had "imagined" she gave me in my meditation. I usually felt that, on some psychic plane, my meditation had helped heal the other person as well as myself.

To do this meditation, you may want to ask a friend to lead you through it, or you can take turns leading one another. This way you will be free to focus on your inner self and trust the other person to steer you back if you get stuck or too far off the track. It will be up to her to keep in mind what the purpose of the meditation is, to use her imagination and sensitivity to ask leading questions, to prod you or support your movement. As you go through the meditation, describe it out loud so that your friend knows what is happening. You can read over the directions in advance and decide if you want to make any changes in them. Pause between directions. The directions that are in parentheses are alternatives that you may want to use. If you want to contact the guide by yourself, read over the directions several times until you have a good understanding of them, or make a tape recording to play to yourself.

• Find some time and space where you can be quiet and undisturbed for about an hour. (A good position for meditation is to sit on a chair with your feet on the ground, your spine free, and your hands resting on your lap. You may want to touch your thumb to your first and second fingers to form a circle. If you are sure you won't fall asleep, you can lie on the floor with your arms and legs uncrossed, your head resting on the ground. These positions assure that your body is open and your spine in a natural position, and your energy and your breathing free.)

• Do a centering meditation. Tell yourself that you are going to meet your guide, that you will always be in contact with yourself, that your guide is waiting to welcome you and is glad you are coming.

• Feel yourself in the room you are now in. Imagine that you get up, go out the door, and are outside. Feel that you are actually making these movements, not that you are watching yourself. Maintain this awareness the whole time. What is it like outdoors? What do you see around you? What does the ground or pavement feel like under your feet? Is it smooth, rough, wet, dry, hard, soft? What sounds do you hear? What smells are there? Continue in your imagination throughout the rest of the meditation.

• Imagine that you start moving down a road or path. What is it like? Gradually feel yourself moving farther and farther away from buildings and people. You come to a forest. You go deeper and deeper into the woods. Notice the sounds, smells, and sights. Are there any animals and birds? How does it feel to be walking in a forest? What season is it? The weather? Time of day or night? What kinds of trees and land are around you? Spend a little while really feeling yourself in this new place and noticing its features. Eventually you come to a clearing in the woods. What is it like there? What is the light like?

• After making yourself familiar with the clearing, look to your right—in your mind's eye—for your guide. She is there waiting to greet you. Sense her in the ways that are easiest for you. If you are a good visualizer, let the visual image appear before you. What is your guide's physical appearance? What is she wearing? What nationality or era is she from? See if you can catch her eye. If you are more sensitive with your ears, listen for your guide's voice to tell you where she is. Or, you may simply *feel* that your guide is there beside you, and know what she is communicating without seeing or hearing. (If you cannot get any sense of your guide's presence, allow an animal to appear. Ask the animal to lead you to your guide. When you reach your guide, thank the animal and make contact with your guide as described above.)

• Ask, aloud or silently, if she is your guide. If she says "yes," ask her name. Exchange greetings and tell your guide how you feel about meeting. (If she says she is not your guide, ask who she is and if she will lead you to your guide. If she refuses, leave and continue to look for your guide, perhaps calling on an animal for help.)

• Ask your guide if she has anything she would like to say to you. You may want to walk around a bit or sit and have a chat. Ask what you can do to open up your inner self and integrate it with your other self. Hold hands with your guide and do anything else that allows the energy to flow between you. Continue to be aware of the setting that you are in and feel yourself actually being there.

• Ask your guide if she has anything more she would like to say. Tell her how you feel about meeting and that you would like to come back. Ask what is the best way for you to do this. When should you come back next? How will you come back— the same way or another? Does she have any suggestions as to what you should do when you come back? Any advice for what you should do in your outside life? Finally, ask your guide for a present, to tell you about its power, and where you should carry it.

• Say goodbye to your guide. Affirm your connection with her with a hug or by holding hands. Make sure you have your gifts with you and remember what has happened. Look around once more at the landscape. Come back through the woods and the road, sensing once more what it is like in there. Gradually, you near your place of origin, and enter it. Feel yourself in there for awhile. When you are ready, start to sense your body as it is in the room. Feel the surface beneath you, your breathing, what your body feels like. Slowly touch yourself all over. When you are ready, slowly open your eyes and bring your consciousness back to the room.

Record in some way the gifts you received, what was asked of you, what you learned, saw, felt. You can write brief notes or a long description of your guide journey. You may want to draw or paint the setting, your guide or other figures, or yourself with your gifts. You may want to make or buy a physical representation of the spirit gifts you received.

NOTES

Hallie's First Guide Meeting (1972)

Here's a description of my first guide meditation:

I am in a cave. The floor is deep underneath my feet. It feels cool in here and I like it. The cave is bare except for some pebbles on the ground. I notice a medium-sized hole to my right. I wriggle through it. It leads to a tunnel that is big enough to stand up in. Being in this tunnel feels pretty secure to me. I wish there were more light, though, and then I notice some lanterns on the wall with matches beside them. I walk down the tunnel, lighting the lanterns as I go. Soon I come to another opening. I step through it.

I am on a cliff in high-altitude desert country, very beautiful, with rocks of all different colors. It is summer, in the early afternoon, very quiet, and I have the sense of something very powerful around me.

I look to the right for my guide. I do not see anyone there, and I try to get a visual image. None comes. I sense that my guide is behind a big boulder to my right. I ask my guide to come out from behind the boulder. Suddenly, a young androgynous figure steps out. S/he has long blond hair, looks fairly modern, and is wearing loose clothing. "Hello, Hallie," s/he says. "I've been waiting a long time for you." I ask her name and s/he says it is Leo. I ask if s/he has a present for me and s/he gives me a beautiful woven belt to wear around my waist so that I will always know that s/he is with me.

I ask Leo to take me to the Sun. We go down a steep gravel path. I have to step carefully to make sure I don't slip. When we get to the bottom, we are in a beautiful, green, grassy meadow with flowers and a flowing stream. It is a different kind of land from up on the cliff, but that's okay. The Sun is sitting on a rock. He is a young man, small and strong. He feels a little unreachable. I ask him what he needs from me. He says he needs me to believe more in myself and to let more yellow into my life. He gives me a golden hoop to pass over my whole body whenever I need strength and centering. I feel the warmth and energy of the hoop shimmering through my whole body, particularly in my chest.

I next ask my guide to take me to see the High Priestess. Leo leads me along a path that goes into the woods. We come to where the High Priestess lives. She is standing outside her house in the woods in a patch of sunlight surrounded by flowers. She is about forty, strong, with long hair, very graceful and powerful. We dance about the woods for a bit. She wants me to realize that whatever I do as a strong woman contributes to feminism, even if I can't directly see the connection. Even if I spend a lot of my time meditating and just living a normal life, I will be filling that part of the world with new ways for women to be. She gives me one of her flowers to wear in my chest to remember how strength and beauty and delicacy can be combined. It is a beautiful pansy. I thank her.

I ask Leo to bring the Sun over so that we can all be together. The Sun and the High Priestess already know one another, but there is an air of tension between them. I ask what they need from me and one another so that we can all work together. The Sun needs me to stop separating the different parts of my life, such as the rational and the intuitive, from one another. He needs the High Priestess to share some of her magic and lightness, for he feels very heavy. The High Priestess wants me to recognize the strength that is already in my life and asks the Sun to shine on her flowers more. They both agree to each other's requests and the air feels a lot lighter and clearer. We have tea together and everyone seems on very good terms. Finally we all hold hands and Leo, the Sun, and I say goodbye to the High Priestess. She tells me I can come back any time I want and that she has a lot of wisdom to share with me. Leo and I take the Sun back to his rock, but he doesn't want to sit on it any more. He decides he will walk around and enjoy the day. We hug goodbye and I thank him for the hoop.

Leo and I climb back up the path. I feel very satisfied, amazed at how much was within me, and a little tired. When we reach the top, I thank Leo. S/he tells me to come back every day for a while if I can and that s/he will introduce me to any other figures that I want. S/he tells me to take it easy and to spend some time when I come out integrating this experience. I thank Leo and we hug.

I come back through the tunnel. It seems a lot easier than when I first came through it and I feel as though I belong here now. The cave is exactly the same as when I left it and I feel grateful to it for helping me take this journey inward. Gradually, I come back to my body and the room in which I'm sitting.*

Group Meditations

Meditating in a group reaches depths and produces experiences different from those I have when I am meditating alone. Group meditation is a classic example of the whole being greater than the sum of all the parts. Each person receives from the collective energy and, at the same time, is a channel for it. The usual distractions are not so noticeable when we are surrounded by others with a similar intent, especially one as focused as meditation. The reinforcement we get from sharing our meditations with others makes our individual experiences more real and acceptable to us, and the connections that we make within the group are invaluable. Relying only on verbal communication can limit a group. When we share our inner selves, we become much closer, can share more, and work together better.

You can get together with a group primarily to meditate, or you can integrate these meditations and those in the rest

---

*For detailed instruction in inner guidework and relating it to the Tarot and astrology, see Edwin C. Steinbrecher, *Inner Guide Meditation* (Northants, England: Aquarian Press Ltd., 1982).

of the book into an existing group, whether it is spiritual or action-oriented. Also, any of the meditations or exercises for individuals can be adapted to a group.

To do a group meditation, choose one person to read the instructions aloud, or take turns reading them to one another. Be sure to allow pauses. Different people have different paces in different meditations. Don't worry if you find that you are ahead of or behind the group. There will always be time for you to wait for them or catch up with them. When you finish a meditation, share what you experienced with one another. You may find that you have similar or identical experiences, or that you can give one another helpful feedback.

The Circle of Hands

An essential part of many Womanspirit meetings is beginning and ending by sitting in a circle and holding hands. When we arrive we are often distracted by the pressure of transportation, schedules, work, and other personal problems. Taking time to consciously connect with one another allows us to re-energize. Even if we arrive feeling fairly centered, meditating together provides a transition so that we can adjust ourselves to being with the group and focus on what it is we are to do together. Each member of the group becomes more centered and, as individual energies merge, the group as a whole has more power. The meetings become more efficient, creative, and enjoyable. A circle of hands is a good centering device any time a meeting becomes too fragmented. Just stop, take the time to refocus in the circle, and disorganization often disappears. At the end of a session, the circle "grounds" the energy so that we can reconnect in a nonverbal way and makes the transition to the rest of our lives.

Before I knew about all the associations of women with circles (such as the womb, the moon, and the circles on women's bodies in Paleolithic and Neolithic cave paintings), a round image would often float into my consciousness when I breathed into my belly. Now I understand how this symbol of wholeness relates to my growing power as a woman, and to my woman's belly. I can develop this symbol as a way of communicating to others how I feel about women, wholeness, and power. I feel the great power of the "Circle of Women," our meeting together and discovering and expressing ourselves.

I worked with a group of four women to prepare psychic action workshops and the closing ritual for the thousand-woman Conference on Violence Against Women that was held in San Francisco in December 1976. We began and ended each of our planning meetings holding hands. Sometimes one of us would spontaneously lead the others through a short breath relaxation. Once we were all so exhausted that we began by lying in a wheel formation with our heads in the center and our hands on each other's bellies. Soon we were all laughing instead of grumbling, relaxed instead of tense. The meetings were quick, clear, and efficient. We usually ended them by simply holding hands and feeling the energy. Each time reminded me how differently I felt from when we had held hands in the beginning, and how much we had accomplished. I often felt amazement at how easy it was to work with these women, even though I didn't know some of them and we had never worked together before. The two general conference coordinators who were responsible for our workshops and attended all our meetings commented on how well our group worked together. Our attention to relaxing first and focusing on letting our energy flow among ourselves made a difference, they thought. We were able to express conflicting opinions, but tried not to let them destroy us.

Some people may feel self-conscious doing this or any other meditation. If you feel reluctant, try allowing yourself to just experiment. Give it a try and see how it makes you feel. Decide beforehand whether you will send energy with your right or left hand, and adapt the directions accordingly.

Here's how to do the circle of hands:

• Sit in a circle and take the hands of the women on either side of you. If there are too many of you to sit in one circle you can sit in concentric circles or crescents. If you have to sit in rows, the women at one end of each row can touch or join hands with the woman in front or back of her until the whole group is connected.

• Close your eyes and take a few deep breaths. Notice how you are sitting. What is your breathing like? Imagine that it travels to any place that you want to release in your body, carrying with it any unnecessary tension. Let yourself settle into the floor, feel your feet or buttocks in contact with it. Notice your legs, pelvis, chest, back, arms, neck, head. Imagine that a cord runs up your spine, goes through the top of your head, and is attached to the ceiling. This cord helps hold you up—you don't have to make any effort. Feel the air cushioning you on all sides. After a couple of moments, turn your attention towards your hands. What do they feel like? Feel or imagine the breath-energy flowing from the hand of the woman on your left into your hand, across your shoulders, and out your right hand into the next woman, who passes it along to the next, and the next, and the next. Become aware of the energy as it flows around the whole circle and through you, around the circle, through you again, continuing. Feel yourself as part of the whole group. Feel the energy moving through any part or parts of your body that need healing. You are feeding one another with your collective energy, soothing, relaxing, healing, energizing. Do any colors, images, emotions arise in your consciousness? When you feel the energy is flowing, let your breath become sound. Let it continue, uniting and weaving with the others to an improvised chanting/singing, creating its own rhythms and tones. Let it gradually become quieter, until you are returned to silence.

• When you are ready, begin to bring your awareness back to your own body and gently release the hands of the women next to you. Open your eyes and look around you. Do you see differently? Look into people's eyes. How does everyone look compared with when you first started? How do you feel?

If you want, instead of holding hands, put your hands on one another's necks, bellies, lower backs, or any other places that would like some energy.

At any time, make up your own version, depending on what you or the group needs at the moment.

Chanting and Music

Music is one of the best part of many religions, and many traditional meditations include everyone's participation in music-making and movement. Powerful words combined with certain rhythms and melodies can transform energy immediately and help open up individual and group consciousness. Holding hands and singing together is a strong group meditation. Improvising with musical instruments, especially simple ones like drums and rattles, helps weave a special energy around the meditation.

• Try starting out with a circle of hands meditation, focusing on the breath. Gradually allow your breath to become sound—any sound: a wordless chant, sounds of nature, emotions—whatever sounds want to come out of you at different moments. If you have instruments, take turns spontaneously playing them, even if you think you don't know how—the energy of the meditation will lead you. Let the blending of the group sound gradually die out. Sit in silence for several more minutes, feeling how the energy in the circle has changed. Tell one another what you experienced.

Here are some songs from women's circles. Most of these songs are widely used in gatherings, and have several different versions. They have become "traditional," in that the names of the individuals or groups who originally evolved them are generally not known and that they often have many different versions. All of them, and others, are important in women's circles.

The Earth, the Air, the Fire, the Water
(Native American Chant—Sung by Women While Grinding Flour)

The earth, the air, the fire, the wa-ter re-turns re-turns re-turns re-turns {the a-
hay a-hay a-hay a-hay a-ho a-ho a-ho a-ho a-HO! *(clap!)*   *shout!*

Each section of this chant is repeated twice. The meter can be changed according to drumming or moving patterns. When singing "earth," hands touch ground; when singing "air," hands move in spirals from earth to sky; when singing "fire," hands motion upwards; when singing "water," hands motion downwards.

Long Wing Feathers
(Native American, Traditional)

I cir-cle a-round, I cir-cle a-round the bound-'ries of the Earth, the bound-'ries of the Earth, wear-ing my long wing feath-ers as I fly, wear-ing my long wing feath-ers as I fly, I

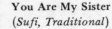

Suggested drum: eight to a measure, accent every fourth beat. Keep a good dance rhythm going.

Repeat as many times as you want. In group singing, a round often develops after a few times through.

The song ends on "Earth"—hold as long as you want.

You Are My Sister
(Sufi, Traditional)

You are my sis-ter, you are my moth-er, you are my lov-er and my friend. You are the cen-ter and the be-gin-ning, you go far be-yond the end. I love you so you help me see see you in all, see you in me. For I'm in you and you're in me, for I'm in you and you're in me. You are my me.

There's a String Through the Center
(Beading Song)

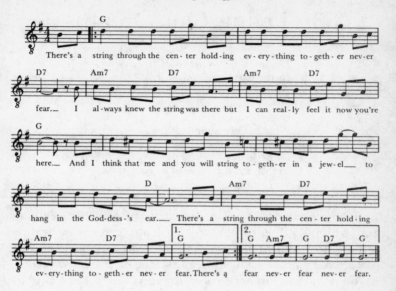

There's a string through the cen-ter hold-ing ev-ery-thing to-geth-er nev-er fear.__ I al-ways knew the string was there but I can real-ly feel it now you're here.__ And I think that me and you will string to-geth-er in a jew-el__ to hang in the God-dess-'s ear.__ There's a string through the cen-ter hold-ing ev-ery-thing to-geth-er nev-er fear. There's a fear nev-er fear nev-er fear.

Sing one octave below written melody.

3. Living Our Dreams

Dreams are the myths of the psyche.
In the early morning—
I wander in the labyrinth
Of my dreams.
O shy dreams
Who will not come out into
The light of day
Or be held by any
But by a touch as light as your own.

Reclaiming our dreams is an essential way for women to tap our wisdom and learn how to create our psyches in healthy ways. One result of the overemphasis on rationality in our patriarchal culture is an unhealthy fear of the unconscious. By denying the importance of dreams, our society cuts us off from an important source of wisdom and personal power. Our lack of understanding of dreams partially explains why a reported two-thirds of the dreams in this culture are unpleasant, why disaster dreams are almost the only recognized precognitive dreams, and why most people have lost touch with the power of their inner lives.

Consider, for example, this dream I had as a child. It is a classic representation of the powerlessness of humans, particularly women and girls, in patriarchal religions:

"I am five years old. My parents are giving a party and my mother and I are in the kitchen. We know that God has ordered us not to say anything to one another. I whisper something to my mother. Suddenly, she and I are whisked to the top of the staircase by an angel. It is dark. I know that my mother and I are going to Hell and it is all my fault."

This nightmare is my earliest childhood memory. It

haunted me for many years. If I had lived in a culture that regarded dreams differently, my family might have led me through a reworking of this nightmare, so that I could communicate more directly with my mother, God, and the angel, find out what they meant to me in my life, and do something to resolve the conflicts that created the dream. But my society told me it was "just a dream" and to forget it. My dreams remained mysteries that fascinated and sometimes terrified me.

Other cultures, in which women's wisdom is recognized, do not treat dreams the way ours does. The Tibetans, for example, often begin mornings with a discussion of dreams in order to integrate into daily life the subconscious wisdom expressed in dreams of the night before. The best-known example of a culture that uses dreams to develop fully integrated personalities is the Senoi. The Senoi are a Malaysian tribal people who are noted for being peaceful, cooperative, and neurosis-free. They are able to achieve these qualities and maintain individualism and creativity by using dreams to plan their lives and to integrate their conscious and unconscious selves into a free, healthy whole. This integration is a major goal of meditation, and working with dreams can be a valuable adjunct to meditation work.

Women and Dreams

Since prehistoric times, women have been associated with the night, darkness, and the unconscious. The moon, a traditional emblem for women, is also associated with dreams, "other worlds," and special powers —as well as with "lunacy." Modern psychology has further reinforced these associations of women with the emotions and the unconscious. It is significant that as women are asserting their political power, dreams and other psychic phenomena are also being reclaimed from centuries of disparagement.

Whether or not women are innately more emotional and attuned to the psyche than men are, we have been brought up to think that we are and have been encouraged to develop our sensitivity in these areas. In an age where psychic phenomena are increasingly recognized, we have a head start.

Although the ancient Greek tragedians, the Bible, Shakespeare, and traditional folk and fairy tales refer to the beauty and power of dreams, as well as to their usefulness in problem solving, creativity, and divination, modern technological culture has been suspicious of any form of "irrationality." Logic is certainly not the only way to gain information or insight; but, as western cultures struggled out of the depths of ignorance and superstition with the help of science, logic began to acquire the air of sacred untouchability once accorded to kings and gods. As technology increasingly dominated and denied natural forces, dreams and other forms of psychic power fell into disrepute.

Modern western psychology arose in an attempt to alleviate the estrangement from our inner selves that resulted from trying to rely entirely on the rational mind. Yet even such an innovator as Sigmund Freud valued dreams primarily as a psychic garbage can, the contents of which were illusionary wish-fulfillments or expressions of neuroses to be rationally dissected, analyzed, and disposed of. Another influential twentieth-century psychologist, Carl Jung, was more accepting of dreams and encouraged his patients to look to their dreams for guidance and inspiration. Yet his categorizations, particularly regarding female "receptivity" and male "assertion," are too limiting for both women and men.

Our society discredits the brilliant, complex, and direct wisdom of dreams. Popular attitudes and education still make it difficult to take dreams seriously and to believe that we can work *with* them, rather than just forget them or be haunted by them. We are brought up to distrust or discount the nonrational as inferior judgment—"That can't be right!

It doesn't make sense" (when often the "sense" doesn't reveal itself rationally until later)— or as self-indulgent—"I just want to believe that."

However, dreams have always inspired people. One of the most famous examples is that of F. A. Kekulé, the nineteenth-century German chemist who discovered the formula for benzene from a dream. He stayed up all night experimenting, inspired by a dream image of a snake swallowing its own tail. This image led him to the structure of the benzene molecule. When I was working on this book, I had dreams in which I thought of a structure and title for the book that was radically different from any I had thought of. I used the ideas from the dreams, which also reminded me to be open to other new ideas. Photographer Marcelina Martin, who took many of the photographs for this book, describes how she uses dreams as a source of creativity:

Through the years I've become more and more involved with art as ritual and the artist as shaman/ritual maker. Many of my images come from guided meditations or dreams. "On The Dreamwheel" came from a dream I had during a time of transition in my life. I was working with the Medicine Wheel, a Native American ceremony. The wheel is a pattern of stones used as a "meditation." I had a dream that I was the hub of the wheel with stones on my face, arms, and hands. I asked a woman to work with me on this dream by posing in a photographic session. I collected small shells at the beach and pasted them on her face, arms, and hands in certain patterns. "On the Dreamwheel" was the most significant photograph to emerge. Not only does the image call up the strength and power that I felt in the dream; it also reminds me that creativity heals.

In recent years, Asian, African, Native North and South American, and Australian forms of dreamwork have been more publicized, as have practices from ancient European cultures that were more attuned to the wisdom of dreams than modern one. In most of these cultures, women's wis-

On the Dream Wheel

dom strongly influences such practices. For instance, in Native American cultures, the dreams of menstruating women are considered to be particularly wise, and these women were consulted by the decision-making elders.

My first experience of Womanspirit dreamwork came when I joined a women's group led by a friend of mine, Alice Abarbanel. At the first meeting, we went around the room and each of us talked about her relationship to her dreams. An overwhelmingly powerful feeling grew in the room as fifteen women, most of whom had never met one another, shared their inner lives. After a few hours had gone by, I felt as though we had spent lifetimes together. We had reached a level of honesty, trust, and intimacy rarely shared, especially by strangers.

Now, individual women dreamers, women's dream groups, and women dream researchers are discovering new ways to live with dreams. Through Womanspirit dream meditation, I began, as an adult, to accept and respect my dreams as important parts of myself and to discover what their inspiring, puzzling, and frightening aspects could teach me. I began to merge my conscious and unconscious selves and learn how to live my dreams. Dealing directly with dream issues helped me confront and resolve parts of my waking life in which I had previously felt powerless. My dreams remind me that there is more to existence than I often realize. They bring me the visions, answers, and beauty I rush past in my daily life. Sometimes dreamwork is my major meditation.

Like many other aspects of Womanspirit meditation, dreamwork is an opportunity to unblock the energy flow between our divided parts, in this case our waking and sleeping selves. As we open the connections between the conscious and unconscious aspects of our beings, we reclaim our spiritual selves from isolation and neurosis.

In Womanspirit dreamwork, we accept our dreams on their own terms and learn how to work with them, trusting our intuitive selves to speak first, with rationality as a strong support. We develop our dreams, complete them, improve them, and manifest them in work, artforms, ideas, and pleasure. As we apply what we learn from our dreams to our work, artistic ventures, political action, and personal growth, we break down yet another barrier, the one that lies between rationality and intuition. By recognizing our dreams as creative sources, and ourselves as talented and productive women, we simultaneously affirm and develop powers that have long been hidden. When we share our dreams with one another, we reach a closeness that transcends the usual physical, psychological, and social separations.

Basic Guidelines

If you decide that you want to work with your dreams, there are some basic guidelines. Decide whether you want to do it alone or with others. You need to do some work on your own, but you can also share dreams with a roommate or partner, form or join a dream group, or spend the night with a group of friends and share your dreams in the morning. Other people will often offer new perspectives and/or encouragement.

An important part of strong dreaming is sleeping well. Create your sleeping space as your own private dream sanctuary. Choose bedding that is comfortable and inviting, whether it be a firm mattress (put a board under it if is too soft), a waterbed, a foam pad, or a futon. If you have trouble going to sleep, try doing breathing and stretching exercises before going to bed, or drinking a relaxing herbal dream tea such as peppermint or camomile.

However you decide to work, congratulate yourself for dreaming! Everyone dreams, whether or not she remembers her dreams. We spend 20 percent of our sleeping hours dreaming, so there is a wealth of dreams for us to tap into. I have heard countless people say "I don't dream" or "I never remember my dreams." These same people find their dreams "coming through" clearly soon after they start working with them.

Tell yourself that you will remember your dreams. Tell yourself throughout the day and before you go to sleep that you will remember your dreams. Do this in the form of a positive statement, such as, "Tonight I will remember my dreams," rather than, "It sure would be nice if I remembered my dreams."

Congratulate yourself for remembering your dreams. Pleasant or unpleasant, your dreams are invaluable guides to your waking and sleeping life. Enjoyable dreams are exciting and creative adventures in which you tap some of your most powerful resources. Unpleasant dreams are your psyche's way of growing, of dealing with the world, and of seeking new knowledge. You can rework them and transform them into enjoyable dreams.

Talk to other people about your dreams. Exploring dreams with other people is an important way of learning to work with dreams. It counteracts the lack of value our society gives them. Dreams are part of our personal mythology, and in sharing them we create a new collective women's mythology, new ways of relating to one another, a new culture, and our own community.* Listen to the other's dreams without imposing your own associations on it. Ask questions to help the dreamer probe deeper, or, when she is finished telling her dreams, offer your intuitive reactions to it.

Pay special attention to dreams at critical times in your life. Your dreams may give you helpful perspectives.

Respect the nightly, seasonal, and lifetime cycles of your dreams. Women's dreams are particularly associated with the menstrual cycle, with dream recall reportedly highest around the time of ovulation. Our natural sleeping rhythms are part of the cycles of our dreams. Exhaustion, drugs, and the morning alarm can inhibit your dream life as well as your waking life. If possible, go to bed before you are too tired, so that you can wake up naturally. You will probably remember more dreams and more details about each dream.

---

*See Chapter 4 for more on personal and collective mythology.

Set aside time for working with your dreams. The best time is when you first wake up. Spend a few minutes lying still and going over your dreams. If you do not remember any dreams or dream fragments, pay attention to your mood or to what you were thinking about when you woke up, or run through the important events of the preceding days. The thoughts or impulses you have upon awakening may lead you to your dreams. After you have remembered as much as you can, change your position or roll over in bed and see if you remember more. It works like magic!

Keep a dream journal. Buy or make yourself a nice dream journal that makes you feel especially good about your dreams. Use one that has blank pages so you can draw when you want. Mine are notebooks covered with a favorite picture or wrapping paper. They are simple, inexpensive, and beautiful—and make wonderful presents.

Record your dreams. As you record them, you will find yourself gradually remembering more dreams and more about each dream. Write your dreams down, draw images or charts of your dreams, make up songs about them, or tape record them. You can use a special pen for writing dreams if you wake up in the middle of the night. They are available from many department stores and have a light in them which illuminates the area on which you are writing.

Keep materials within easy reach. I keep my notebook and pen by my pillow. If you have many long dreams, make a few notes about them when you first wake up, so that they don't slip away while you are recording the details of your first dreams. As you begin to record your dream, you will remember more about it. If you work with an inner guide, going through your dream with your guide will often help you remember large portions of dreams.

Use the present tense when you describe or record your dream. This will help you relive the dream as much as possible. Feel yourself as you were in the dream. Feel your actions, your emotions, your attitude. Also note colors, variations in energy and movement, and other less concrete aspects of your dream. If the dream is particularly vivid or schematic you may want to draw images from it or make a map of it.

Sometimes a dream can be best expressed visually. Keep colored pencils or felt tip pens with your dream materials so that you can record images, colors, and movement that you see in your dreams. For a particularly powerful dream image, set aside time to create your own masterpiece. Creating artwork from dreams, whether it be painting, photography, embroidery, sculpture, or leatherwork, is a good meditation for reclaiming creative skills. Trust the imagery and don't judge it with your critical, logical mind. Create spontaneously—the images will lead *you*. My art is quite primitive, and the simplicity allows the power of the vision to shine through.

A good way to focus your dream meditations is by making a dream pillow. Take whatever material seems most evocative of dreams and sew a small bag, stuffing it with mugwort (for strong dreaming) and psyllium seeds (for helping in remembering dreams). You can get these herbs from most health food stores. The meditation of making the pillow will help direct your attention and the herbs will affect your consciousness, particularly if you sleep with the pillow.

Allow for changes. As you work with your dreams, your relationship with them will change and grow. After a year and a half of writing down my dreams every morning (three to six dreams each day) and working with them, I suddenly got very tired of doing it. It took me awhile to feel that it was okay to let go of working with my dreams so deliberately. Then I realized that even though I wasn't working with all of them, they were integrating themselves into my waking life without my conscious effort. I would often wake up from my dreams with my energy clear and ready for what-

ever I needed to do that day. During the period I wrote this chapter, I went back to writing down my dreams and working directly with them. I found that since my time away from them, my dreams have become more exciting than they were before, and my dreaming and waking decision making, creativity, and assertiveness have all grown. I realized that *not* working with my dreams is sometimes as beneficial as working with them.

Practical Advice

When working with your dreams, look to see if they are offering you any practical advice. Your unconscious mind may be giving you information that your conscious mind is unaware of or has not taken enough notice of. A practical dream may have other layers as well.

For instance, a few years ago I dreamed about a drought. Awake, I realized that my haphazard method of watering my plants was turning into neglect and that some were dying. In addition, at the time of my dream there was a severe drought of several years throughout California and I knew my dream reflected my concern with the lack of rain. On a psychic level, I realized that large parts of my life were not getting enough "water" or care.

At another time, I started having a series of dreams about ballet schools, dance performances, and water ballet. I had known that I wanted to take a dance class for excercise and to develop my physical self and confidence. The dreams showed me that this was an important new part of my life and, encouraged by them, I signed up for a theater class and a tumbling class. These classes opened a whole new chapter in my life, helping me to discover the clown and dancer in me.

Ann Hershey had this dream while we were working with dreams in a Womanspirit relationship class. In waking life, she was struggling with letting go of her idea of what a particular relationship should be like:

"I am holding a round, clear ball. Two spirit guides, on either side of me, are trying to show me how to use it so that I can see the future and find answers to my questions. They show me that if I let go, the ball floats just in front of me and the answers appear in the globe. I am afraid it will fall and keep trying to hold on to it. I find that if I let go of it, it does float but as soon as I grab it and try to hold it, it drops to the earth, weighted and heavy."

Recreating Dreams

One of the most basic and profound ways of working with dreams is to recreate them—in a meditation similar to a fantasy or making up a story, as part of inner guidework (see Chapter 2), or with another person leading you through the dream reworking. The guideline for recreating your dreams is: "What do I want to do in this dream?" It's your dream and you can do what you want in it and change it in any way you want! Most people begin by reworking their dreams when they are awake. After a while, many find that they become conscious in a dream and can redirect the action as they please. Others may wake up, go back to sleep, and dream a new, more satisfactory version of the dream.

I learned to do dream re-creation in Alice Abarbanel's ongoing group, in which we simulated a Senoi family and guided one another through meditations to rework our dreams. This group focus intensified the power of changing my dream and waking life, for the attention of so many people gave me added strength and imagination.*

In my classes, I found that women need extra encouragement in dealing with confronting difficult and violent characters in dreams. Our dream selves are victimized psychologically and physically: we are subjected to an array of attacks ranging from mild confusion to rape and murder. When we substitute new responses and possibilities in our meditations and dreams, we can gradually change our attitudes and actions in waking life.

---

*I later discovered the "Senoi checklist" in Patricia Garfield's *Creative Dreaming* (New York: Simon and Schuster, 1974) and found it a helpful tool.

Our usual reaction to dreams in which we are bothered, harassed, or attacked by an emotion, situation, person, animal, or other figure is to reassure ourselves that "it was just a dream" and to try to forget about it as quickly as possible. Since doing this prevents us from completing the dream energy satisfactorily, we are often haunted by the dream or the discomfort it leaves behind. We do not have to be victims. A dream situation or figure is threatening only as long as the dreamer feels it to be. Our fear gives power to dream aggressors. When we confront them or unmask them, they lose this negative power and we transmute it into positive energy, either in the dream itself or by releasing energy in our waking lives. Violence is a human potential, but if we choose to deal with it on the dream level, we may defuse it before it manifests itself physically.

Many women hesitate to be violent in their dreams or in reworking them. We have been taught to be nice and, in addition, we know what it feels like to be threatened by violence. In Womanspirit groups, women find that as they practice confronting harassment and violence in reworking their dreams they become more assertive when awake. This in turn gives them more strength in their dreams, which in turn gives them more strength in waking life, as the unconscious, or dream life, is a rehearsal for daily life.

Choose a dream that you want to change. Find a quiet place and time (about fifteen to thirty minutes). If you can, rework the dream as soon as you remember it when you wake up. If you work with an inner guide, ask your guide to help you. Imagine yourself as you were in the dream. What is the setting? What are the smells? Colors? Sounds? What are you doing? What are you thinking? Feeling?

Rework the dream using the present tense. Feel yourself actually there. You can ask anything you want of the figures. If they're new or disguised figures, ask, "Who are you and what do you represent to me?" Ask any dream figure about its role in the dream ("Why did you do that?" "What does it mean?") if that is puzzling to you. You can also ask it about any part of the dream or any aspect of your waking life that seems relevant. You can try imagining that you are the dream figure, and from that perspective, reveal the message.

Change the action of the dream in any way that you would like. You can fly to new lands and explore them, open doors that are locked, and discover new friends and lovers.

If a dream figure (individual, situation, atmosphere) is bothering you in any way, turn on it and confront it either in the dream or in a waking meditation. If it is amorphous, ask it to take a form. Try to negotiate with it into a friendly exchange. Ask it what it represents. If necessary, tell it to stop bothering you. Try overwhelming it with love. If all else fails, and a difficult character refuses to cooperate/ negotiate, fight with it, call upon dream or waking friends to help you. Subdue it. If necessary, kill it and allow it to be reborn as a benevolent figure. Remember that, in dreams, death— even your own—is often a necessary step in psychic rebirth. You can judge what you want to change.

Continue the dream reworking *until it feels complete* and you are satisfied. Review your gifts, what you have learned, and how it can carry over into your waking life.

If any part of your dream has to do with a person in your waking life, carry your dream out on that level. Tell the person about the dream, or if that is not appropriate, change your interaction with the person as the dream or dream reworking suggests.

NOTES

As you practice re-creating your dreams, you will find that you can consciously direct your life more than before. You may even remember this while dreaming. This is something I never thought would happen to me. Nevertheless, here is a dream I had while writing this chapter:

Asleep: I am being chased along a country road by two men I knew in high school. I know that they are trying to rape me. I see a steep road going down into a farm at the bottom of a canyon and start to run down it. I realize with horror that there's no escape there: the road dead ends at the farm, the men will probably catch up with me before I get to the bottom, and even if I get to the bottom, other men will be waiting there who will help rape me. As I am running along, I suddenly realize, "I don't have to put up with this!" I stop, turn on the rapists, and make them dematerialize.

Planning Your Dreams

You can consciously direct the content of your dreams to a particular subject: a solution to a problem, a creative project or special guidance. Dreams can indicate the best course of action by presenting it favorably, or the dynamics of a dream may reveal the underlying influence of a situation. Sometimes your sleeping mind allows blockages to disintegrate during the night, so that when you wake up in the morning you simply "know" what to do, even if you don't remember a specific dream.

When I began to be conscious of dreamwork, I realized that I often dreamed about what I had been reading about just before I went to sleep. I decided I didn't want to influence my dreams by media—I wanted to dream about my own life. I decided not to read late at night, or to be more selective about it. I discovered that if, instead, I spent that time reviewing my day, I could pick out areas that seemed unresolved and look at their various aspects as I was falling asleep. Then I would dream about the person or situation and, when awake, could see elements that I had ignored or not dealt with.

If I had a decision to make that I couldn't resolve, I would focus on it before I went to sleep, telling myself that my sleeping mind would give me the answer and that I would trust my dream or my first waking feelings. When I woke up, I immediately asked myself, "What shall I do?" Either I remembered a dream that clearly showed me the answer, or I had a strong feeling about what was best. Sometimes I had to discipline myself to trust my intuition and not fall back into doubt and rationalizations.

• If you want to plan your dreams, get a definite idea of what you want. Make up a simple sentence or phrase describing what you will dream about, such as, "Shall I take this job?" This gives your dream self a clear message and makes it easier for you to focus on your project both when you are awake and asleep.

• Spend waking time occupied with the subject that you want to dream about; think, meditate, read, talk, go to museums, movies, etc. The material needs varying lengths of time to incubate within you, filter down through the many layers of your consciousness, integrate with other elements, and re-emerge in your dream consciousness in its new form—much as a seed needs time to mingle with the earth, minerals, and water before growing and blooming.

• Spend time just before you go to sleep reading, thinking, or meditating on your chosen subject. A good method is to spend fifteen to twenty minutes writing down as many different aspects of the situation as you can think of: the problems, the good points, possible stumbling blocks, hopes, expectations, and so on. Then formulate a clear phrase or image that summarizes the situation. As you are going to sleep, focus on the phrase or image so that you can deal directly and clearly with the problem.

• When you wake up, even if it is the middle of the night, examine all your dreams, waking ideas, attitudes, and moods. Record all dreams immediately. If you wait, you may totally forget them or lose some of that indefinable quality that makes creative dream images so powerful. If you are working on a creative project, sometimes it is better to focus on it as soon as you wake up, even if it means not writing down and meditating on your dreams in the usual way. When I was writing this book, if I went straight to the typewriter when I woke up, working often came much more easily. Even though most of my dreams were not specifically about the writing, the creative energy of the dreams was channeled directly into my work.

• Act on your decision, paint your creation, sing it, laugh it, perform it. Share it with your friends, your coworkers, the rest of your waking life—and ask them to share theirs.

• Form a dream meditation group in which to share your dreams and the creations that come out of them on an ongoing basis.

N O T E S

Working with Others

Sharing our dreams with friends, lovers, or family in our waking lives can be an extremely valuable bridge between our conscious and unconscious selves. Although our dreams are intensely personal and unique creations, other people play important parts in them. In waking life, they can offer insights and help guide us through dream meditations. Working with a dream group allows the whole group to focus on one person's dream. The union of individuals, particularly in Womanspirit work, is far greater than the sum of the parts. The closeness and understanding that result when people help one another psychically carry over into the rest of one's life. I have seen lifelong friendships and partnerships result from each of my groups. When people do Womanspirit work together, they reach closeness and acceptance with one another that few of us know in other relationships.

You can do dreamwork with people you live with, work with, see socially, or contact through bulletin boards, ads, or other notices. Set aside time daily or weekly to share dreams. Lead one another through the dream meditations, feeling free to trust your intuition in creating your own form of dreamwork.

Dancing the Dream Wheel

One of the most comprehensive ways to work with a dream is one in which we all contribute to one dream, just as the spokes of a wheel feed into the hub. To do this, gather a group, bring objects and costumes for props, or use whatever is available. The dreamer tells a dream that she would like to change. She chooses different people in the group to take different roles in the dream. The characters may be people, animals, objects, or even a mood or atmosphere. A few people might be chosen to be a chorus that plays music or makes up chants for the dream.

• All members of the group hold hands quietly for a beginning meditation, asking that each person be able to set aside individual ego and personality for awhile to let whatever guidance needs to come through to help complete the dream in the best way for the dreamer. When you are ready:

• Begin to reenact the dream, as the dreamer told it. At some point, any one character spontaneously begins to change the flow of the enactment (as in a theater improvisation) in a way that would help the dreamer in her confrontation. For instance, a supporting character might urge the dreamer to confront a difficult character, or the difficult character might become more aggressive or passive. All other characters respond accordingly, using their own intuition to help the dreamer act out the dream until it feels completed. Usually it is clear to all when the dream reworking is finished, although the dreamer will determine this.

• When you are finished, share your experience, and close with a circle of hands.

My experience with this form of dreamwork is that, more than in any other meditation, we all become the teacher, for a large amount of respect and trust is needed to give over the direction of the enactment to a spontaneous group process. The results are always brilliant, and the dreamer finds herself with new possibilities she had never considered before. She also learns that her dream can become real, and the other women usually find they are resolving parts of their own dreams at the same time.

Sleeping in a Dream Wheel

Sleeping together and sharing dreams is a powerful tool for dream work and community creating.* You can try this experiment even if you have not been working on your dreams, for it often is a way to facilitate dreamwork.

Invite a group of friends over to spend the night at a time when you can all be free the next morning. Decide whether you all would like to concentrate on dreaming about the

---

*A book that may stimulate your dreaming and your work with a community is Dorothy Bryant's *The Kin of Ata Are Waiting for You* (Berkeley: Moon Books/Random House, 1976).

same thing, or whether your goal will be to enhance your dreams by sleeping together and sharing your dreams in the morning. Tell people to bring bedding, dream notebooks, and drawing materials, and ask them to focus on the individual and collective purpose. Find a place where you can all sleep in the pattern of a wheel, with either all your heads or all your feet facing the center of the wheel. Your bodies will become the spokes of the wheel.

When you meet, spend at least two hours before you go to sleep sitting in your dream wheel together, focusing on your dreams. Sing, make dream pillows, talk about dreams and dream techniques, or share your ideas about what you would like to dream about.

The next morning, each person may write or draw her dreams. If someone does not remember her dreams, she can write or draw how she was feeling when she woke up, for our dreams often manifest themselves in this more subtle way. You may have simple food available so that those who need to can eat a little without disturbing the others' concentration.

When everyone has had time to record her dreams, share them. Pay quiet and close attention to everyone's dream, for they are all the dreams of each member of the dream wheel. Close by holding hands and affirming your ability to make your dreams your own.

Living My Dream

I'd like to share a dream I had in 1970, for it presaged a decade of growth and community that I had no experience of at the time. I had this dream at one of the most frightening and difficult times in my life, and it helped give me enough hope and courage to continue on my search. Since then, I have gone through many such transitions and come to a place where I realize I am truly living my dream:

I am walking along and I come to a hedge like the one I played near when I was little and whose branches I used to make bows and arrows. I discover that there is a hole in the hedge, and I crawl through it. When I come out on the other side, I am in a world inhabited by wonderful people who are all waiting for me. They are dressed in bright, free-flowing clothes, like jesters. I understand instantly that each one puts all of his or her energy into being or making one particular thing, and then shares it with everyone else.

A woman hands me a card she has painted in glowing colors. It is like a medieval Tarot card in its richness, yet it is decorated with my personal symbols and scenes. One man makes beautiful, intricate embroidered bags, filled with all the magic that he knows. He gives me one. Two other people are dressed up like a horse, rearing and dancing gracefully towards me.

I am aware of two striking aspects of this world. First, each person puts all of her or his creativity and magic into what they make. Because they are all clear people, with all their energy flowing freely, what they create and who they are is extremely powerful. And then, each person gives away what she or he has made, with no attachments, but with even more energy and love. This is a totally self-sufficient society, with everyone's physical, emotional, and psychic needs not only satisfied, but lavished upon in a rich and wondrous way.

I think to myself, "This is a really wonderful place. I'll have to remember how I got here, so I can come back again."

And then I realize that I will never leave. I have come through the hole in the hedge, and the world I came from is a faint shadow now. I will never go back again.

Lullaby

Good night
Sleep tight
Dream on
Dream well.

4. Collective and Personal Mythology

> I am Nature, the Universal Mother, mistress of all
> the elements, primordial child of time, sovereign of
> all things spiritual, queen of the dead, queen also of
> the immortals, the single manifestation of all gods
> and goddesses that are. . . . Though I am worshiped
> in many aspects, known by countless names, and
> propitiated in all manner of different rites, yet the
> whole round earth venerates me.
>
> APULEIUS, second century A.D.

Just as working with our dreams can help change our waking and sleeping realities, examining and reshaping our collective mythology and our own individual personal mythologies can also affect our self images and how we act in the world.

Collective Mythology

Collective myths, including fairy tales and folktales, often originate in historical events and people. More universal themes and attributes are added to the stories as time goes by. As such, these myths are the repository for the wisdom and values of a given culture. They are like dreams because they both feed and are fed by the collective unconscious, yet they also express externally imposed values and systems. Reclaiming collective myths that have been distorted by centuries of patriarchy and creating our own myths connects us to our heritage, our own strength, and our own beauty.

Through collective mythology, we can touch the lives of

prepatriarchal peoples in a deep and timeless way. Myths are more than just nice stories for children. They are condensed stories of active, powerful, and wise women. The lives and values of people thousands of years ago and thousands of miles away leap out from the pages. Through the myths, the inner workings of their souls, as well as the reality of their day-to-day lives, speak to us. Like the art from women's cultures, we can react to myths intuitively and emotionally, and their messages can be understood immediately by children and adults. Collective myths can take us deep into the collective and individual psyches of our predecessors and ourselves.

Since mythology expresses the value system of a culture, it simultaneously conditions a person's attitudes and behavior. Because they are often simple and beautiful, because we hear them as children, and because they often describe rewards and punishments, myths are a powerful influence on our actions and values. Just as myths simultaneously reflect and affect our attitudes, so a people's psychology, affected by myths, mirrors and helps determine its politics, economics, and social attitudes. Whether a group is peaceful or warlike, communal or competitive, sexist or egalitarian, whether it embraces nature or relies on technology, is reflected in, and in turn influenced by, its mythology.

Mythmakers thus have a great deal of power over people's lives. The earliest mythmakers were most likely women, and the earliest myths we know of are about women-goddesses, as shown in this quote from a paper my mother, Harriet Iglehart, wrote in 1975 to complete her bachelor's degree:

Among the many myths which originated in ancient times within the Fertile Crescent in the Near East, three Creation Myths serve to form an outline of greatly simplified time periods and religious concepts, and point up the changes in the role of the feminine in mythology and the status of women in the societies. This first is the "Pelasgian Creation Myth," in which Eurynome, the

Goddess of All Things, rises up from Chaos and creates Sea and Sky so she has something to dance on. She then creates the great serpent Ophion by rubbing the North Wind. In time, she becomes a dove and lays the Universal Egg on the ocean. She orders Ophion to coil round it, and from this egg all of nature is born. Later Ophion claims to be the creator of the universe, and Eurynome exiles him.

A second great Creation Myth is the patriarchal myth of Uranus, which was the official creation myth of the Olympian religious system. In this story, Mother Earth emerges from Chaos while asleep, and gives birth to her *son* Uranus. There is a relatively passive creation. He then impregnates her with rain and she produces plants, animals, and birds.

The third creation myth is the Judeo-Christian version; in which a male God creates heaven and earth and a man "in his own image," and later on a woman from the man's rib, naming her after man. . . .

Well, no matter, "in the beginning," there *was* the Great Goddess —whether she be known as Eurynome, Gaia, Ge, The Great Minoan Goddess, or even in her more divided forms—such as Pandora, Themis, Rhea and Kore. The "beginning" means the Paleolithic and Neolithic Ages—the furthest back in time that archaeologists can take us. Women need a new mythology, one that we can relate to. What it means to be a woman today is transforming rapidly, and our psychological, cultural and political changes will be, like those of the ancients, reflected in myths. There is a real need, both for women and men to return to "the Great Time," a need to rediscover pre-patriarchal representation of women and new images of women.

As in these creation myths, the rivalry between goddesses and gods in Greek and Roman myths reflects the conflicts that occurred during the change from matrifocal to male-dominated cultures. Reading about women and goddesses of the past is important as a metaphorical and historical record of woman's power. Myths also give us clues to their predecessors—stories that reflect the significance of strong, independent women in ancient history and prehistory. For instance, when I was little, I could never understand why the Golden Calf in the Bible was destroyed because it was an idol. I saw many people kneel down to the crucifix in my church. From my studies, I now understand that cows have been associated with goddesses for thousands of years and that the Golden Calf destroyed in the Old Testament was one of the representations of women's power.

Luisah Teish describes similar changes in African and Afro-American folktales:

Because of their simplicity and their grounding in natural phenomena, folktales are highly adaptable and travel easily. Thus, in transition, the African jackal becomes the American fox and the forests of the Congo become the Swamps of Louisiana. But this adaptability has its price. Scholars lose much of their original meaning in the translation from one language to another. Oftimes inorganic elements are added. The tales, like people, become taint- ed by racism, elitism, and misogyny.

As a child my mother imparted to me many classical Afro-American tales. All in the first person. She brought each tale to life by naming local streets, using familiar language and addressing im- mediate problems. The test of my intelligence was measured by my ability to decipher these tales and to apply their coded wisdom to my life problems.

The Storyteller has a political obligation to use the *Nommo* (the power of the Word) as a tool for liberation and a channel to world peace. As a black feminist-spiritualist I have accepted the respon- sibilities of this Office, inherited from my mother. I have under- taken the task of turning the African and Afro-American folktales known to me over to the commonsense practice of my mother. I have kept their basic structure, elaborated on their content and substituted outdated images and attitudes with contemporary aspi- rations.

In his book *Los Caracoles*,* Andreas Rogers gives us the story of Ode the Hunter, which is supposed to explain the origin of Women's Menses:

"Ode the Hunter lived with his wife. He always put the blood of

---

*Andreas Rogers, *Los Caracoles: Historia de sus Letras* (Washington, D.C.: Rico Publishing, 1973), p. 70.

the animals at the foot of a tree so Olofi, the Sun, could drink it. His wife asked him why he brought home bloodless animals. He told her to mind her own business and she shut up.

"One day she put three holes in his hunting bag, filled it with ashes and followed his trail to the hunt. She hid behind a bush to watch his actions. When the Sun came to claim the sacrificial blood he saw the woman and said: 'Listen, you, peeking over there, if blood is what you want to see, you will have it forever.' And so Woman was cursed with a period."

Since we know that folklore creates itself from the observance of Nature, this tale is clearly a perverted attempt to explain the incredible phenomenon of Woman's Blood. This tale must be turned around, subjected to natural wisdom: Ode the Hunter associated the loss of blood with death. If an animal bled continually it died, if a *man* bled continually he also died. Yet the wife of Ode bled monthly and *did not* die. He could not fully understand this power and in awe and fear declared it a curse and excluded her from his blood-letting ritual, the Ritual of Death—the Hunt. That Ode the Hunter was sacrificing to the male-identified Sun puts his tale in contraposition to the worship of the Moon which regulates Women's Menstrual Cycle and the Ritual of Life—Childbirth.

Our ancestors created these tales in order to give their descendants the best information/education available at that point in human evolution. Storytellers of today must do the same by reconciling the beliefs of the ancients with modern scientific fact. As an Ancestress of Tomorrow, it is my Sacred Responsibility to leave for my descendants those stories which best illuminate the Spiritual, Social, and Political attitudes of my era. I urge parents (and we are *all* co-parents of Eartha's children) to expose their children to the best of tales, and I urge children to create tales for their Times.*

According to Charlene Spretnak, author of *Lost Goddesses of Early Greece:*

It seems that the origin of goddess spirituality in the Upper Paleolithic era lay in the power of real women, which was both mundane and awesome. Women's bodies bled in rhythm with the

*Luisah Teish, from a work-in-progress, *The Calabash of Memories.*

moon, *produced people,* and transformed food into milk for the young they drew out of their bodies. An additional mystery was that women could produce both women and men. We can't know the thought modes of our Paleolithic ancestors, but we do know that paternity was not recognized for a long time, and it's thought that the elemental power of the female was expressed as the original deity, the Great Mother, worshipped as the source of life.

Later on, as society evolved, the powers associated with the Goddess also evolved, and She became the Divine Ancestor, the Source of Prophecy, the Giver of Divine Wisdom and Just Law. In the later stages of goddess mythology, Her powers became divided among derivative goddesses, as the people in particular geographic areas came to emphasize certain of Her attributes and to call Her by their own name. All of the goddesses in the polytheistic era, though, were derived from Her.

Evidence of goddess-oriented cultures has been discovered in most areas of the world. In Old Europe, that is, Europe prior to the first wave of Indo-European invaders from the Eurasian steppes in c. 4500 B.C., the cultures were spiritually oriented, revered the Earth, produced sophisticated art, and appear to have lived in peace. No fortifications have been unearthed in the many settlements of Old Europe prior to the invasions and the Bronze Age. Also, their burial practices were egalitarian until the Indo-Europeans arrived and enforced their chieftain system. The archaeologist Marija Gimbutas has assembled a great deal of the findings in *Goddesses and Gods of Old Europe, 6500–3500 B.C.**

Naturally, any group that moves into an area and seeks to control it, such as the Indo-Europeans and later the Catholic Church, usually tries to incorporate some of the cultural system they find so that they can make converts more easily. The Indo-European invaders of Greece didn't say, "From now on, we forbid you to ever mention your goddesses again." Instead, they retained the names of most of the pre-Hellenic goddesses, but established their patriarchical gods in command and portrayed the formerly wise, powerful, and compassionate goddesses as mischievous, quarrelsome, perverse, subjugated creatures.

---

*Marija Gimbutas, *Goddesses and Gods of Old Europe, 6500–3500* B.C.: *Myths and Cult Images* (London and Berkeley: Thames & Hudson/ University of California Press, 1974).

Hera is a good example of a goddess who resisted such coopta-
tion. She was a widely revered goddess who had been very important long before the Olympian gods were devised around the
invaders' thunderbolt god, Zeus. In the Olympian system of mythology, however, we know her only as the wife of Zeus, and she is
changed into a bitchy, quarrelsome shrew. This was a radical revi-
sion because she was never anyone's *wife*, nor was she at all petty-
minded and dependent in her original myths. In Olympian mythology their marriage is never smooth; Zeus can never really colo-
nize Hera. It's been pointed out by Jane Ellen Harrison, professor
of classics at Cambridge University at the beginning of the century,
that this myth, the story of the native queen who was conquered
but never subdued by the invaders, is a historical reference to the
resistance to the forced merging of the older pre-Hellenic culture
with the new, patriarchal, warrior-oriented culture of the Indo-
Europeans.

In Christianity there are a lot of clues that indicate that the Virgin Mary was a descendent of the goddess tradition. She produced
her child parthenogenetically as all the other early goddesses had
done, and, like the Near Eastern goddesses, the son she produced
was mourned once a year and was later reborn.*

Tracing the story-myth of Cinderella also reflects the
changing societal roles of women. We find our modern-day
Cinderella in television commercials. As always, she is in her
kitchen, despairing. This woman is completely isolated, all
her energy focused on a task of mythical proportions: making everything about her clean and antiseptic. She is saved
by the White Knight, who materializes, through no action of
her own, and gives her the very cleanser she needs to make
her kitchen as white as he is.

Taking some giant steps backwards in time, we find the
Cinderella of the fairy tale. She is also stuck in the kitchen,
longing to go to the ball and meet the handsome prince, but
this time she is helped by animals or a fairy godmother. (It

---

*Charlene Spretnak, personal communication, 1977. See also Geoffrey
Ashe, *The Virgin* (London and Henley: Routledge & Kegan Paul, 1976), on
the Goddess and the Virgin Mary.

is interesting to note that in the version of the tale told by the Brothers Grimm in the early nineteenth century, it is Cinderella's devotion to her dead mother that helps her. The fairy godmother, a later addition, removes Cinderella from her earthly connections with her biological mother.) She is persecuted by her stepmother and stepsisters, almost ignored by her father, and saved by a prince. This fairy tale describes a male-dominated society in which women are rivals with one another and helplessly dependent upon men for material and psychological security.

Back even further, in the period of the Greek and Roman myths, our Cinderella is one of the many goddesses—say, Persephone, who is raped and abducted by Hades, god/prince of the underworld. Her "fairy godmother" is her mother, Demeter, the goddess of the harvest, who forbids new life to grow until her daughter is returned in a festival of spring. From then on, Persephone divides her time between Demeter and Hades. Such goddesses as Demeter rule over various areas of life, and there is continuous quarreling between the goddesses and the gods. The gods usually win in these stories, yet we can see how hard they have to fight to usurp female power.

Finally, far back in the prehistoric pre-patriarchal period, the earliest period of human existence for which we have evidence, we find no gods, no heroes, but only our kitchen Hera's great-great-great-great-grandmother, the Great Goddess. She is the pre-Hellenic Mediterranean Gaia, Mawu of the Fon of Dahomey, the Egyptian Nut, the Sumerian Nammu, the Assyro-Babylonian Ishtar, the Finnish Virgin of the Air, and the Chinese Kuan-Yin. She alone creates the universe, she alone knows the secrets of life, she alone produces a world that is harmonious and abundant. Her stories are a reflection of a time when women's ability to create physical and psychic life was revered, and when neither women nor men exercised oppressive power over one another, animals, or the earth.

Using Personal Mythology to Create New Mythology

Exploring Your Personal Mythology

Each of us has a personal mythology that shows the patterns and themes in her life and explains how she got to be who she is. This mythology may be presented in the form of stories, songs, pictures, poems, dreams, rituals, objects, or symbols that have special meaning for us and represent important parts of our lives. Some of our personal myths are the tales that all our friends have heard at least once. Whatever form our personal myths take, they draw together resonant threads of our beings, presenting in a unified way a lifetime of values and experiences. Recognizing the mythic aspects of our lives helps us value them more and take more power and responsibility in our lives.

Times are changing rapidly, and the mythologies of twenty years ago, much less two thousand years ago, do not always explain our present reality or help us live in it. Despite their inappropriateness, we often unconsciously live out these myths, even if our rational minds know that we live in a very different world.

This era is a time of consciousness-raising— of all kinds; a time to create *consciously* the myths we want to live by. By recognizing our personal mythologies and developing new mythologies, we can take charge of our lives and our world. An integral part of reclaiming our power as women is acknowledging the new women's mythology and ourselves as mythmakers. We need a mythology of wholeness, one that enriches and stimulates our meditations and self-images. We need a new mythology that tells of strong women, of union with nature, and of cooperation among people. Women have been quiet and have been kept quiet for too long. Our voices are needed to re-establish the balance. As we create a new mythology, we give birth to a new world and, in such deep meditation, give birth to new parts of ourselves. As we create a new world, the new mythology is born.

Just as ancient myths were originally the stories of real people, so our stories will some day be ancient mythology, and future peoples will look to them for information about our values, our everyday lives, the structure of our societies, and the state of our psyches.

Women, being so alienated from the old mythology, have a good chance of creating a new, more satisfying mythology. We need to express stories of women who are free, strong, wise, and self-determining. This mythology is our *own* stories of our lives, not a patriarchal version of what our lives *should* be like. By consciously creating our own mythology, we can gradually change the political and economic realities of our society, as well as changing ourselves.

As we tell our stories, we hear repeated elements that we can all relate to: stories of women finding their strength, discovering their own beauty, and finding other women as sisters, mothers, and daughters through the process of claiming our personal and collective power. We are drawn together as each of us tells her own myths, for we recognize ourselves in one another's trials and joys. Our stories are inspiration for ourselves and one another, as new ways of living and creating. We become our own role models.

Take some aspect of your life and tell it or describe it through words, song, movement, pictures, or whatever. It may be a favorite "true story," a person important to you, or an object that you have powerful associations with. One way to begin to discover your mythology is to go around your house and look at personal objects—artwork, photographs, books, tools, instruments, clothes—noticing associations, stories, emotions, or inspirations that emerge for you. These are part of your personal mythology.

As your personal mythology begins to emerge for you, surround yourself with it. Live it, paint it, sing it, wear it, dance it. Put up pictures that represent your own inner parts. As you do so, allow your mythology to grow, both within you and in your contact with the rest of the world.

Gradually, our new mythology will replace the old.

Think of one incident or area of your life that is problematic for you now. Tell, write, act out, sing, draw, or otherwise express, the story. Then describe the same story in the form of a myth, fairy tale, or folktale. Talk about yourself in the third person. You may want to begin with "Once upon a time. . . ." Maintain the objectivity, as well as the empathy, you would have if you were recounting a story you had read or heard. Recognize the universal themes of your story. Now recreate the same story, still using the myth/fairy tale/folktale format, this time showing how the main character (yourself) uses her intelligence, power and/or love to change the story so that it turns out best for all concerned. Record your new story in words, pictures, songs, and the like. Find ways to integrate your new vision in your everyday life. For example, you might imagine yourself being, acting and thinking differently, according to your new insights.

NOTES

Woman-Line Meditation

Visual and performance artist and workshop leader Betsy Damon created this woman-line meditation. Your woman-line can be your biological forebears, or those women who raised you and their predecessors. Have someone read it to you or your group, tape it, or memorize it for yourself.

Close your eyes and do a relaxation exercise, such as tensing and releasing different parts of your body, or imagining that your breath releases different tensions. When your mind and body feel clear, and you are ready, imagine that you get up, leave where you are, and follow a path to a meadow. Notice everything in your meadow: the time of year, colors, sounds, temperature, and so on.

From this meadow you will be going on a long journey. You will discover your woman-line. They are known and available to you, waiting for you at the edge of the meadow. Go meet them. Beginning with your mother, grandmother, and or other familiar women, you are lifted up and passed back, supported by many women's hands. These hands pass you back 50 years, 100 years, 200 years, 500 to 700 years, 1000 years, 2000 years, even 5000 years, back to the end of your woman line. At the end you arrive at a place, are put down and greeted by a guide. This person will be with you while you spend a day exploring this place. Notice every detail: what it looks like, what is happening. You may ask your guide questions.

At the end of the day and night, get ready to leave. Your guide gives you a gift and returns you to your woman-line. They pick you up, and many hands pass you forward: 5000 years, 2000 years, 1000 years, 500, 300, 200, 100 years, 50 years, until you are once more back in the meadow. Thank them, look around at your meadow once more, and go back along the path. When you are ready, stretch your body and slowly open your eyes.

NOTES

Working in Groups

The Personal Becomes Collective

An important part of our collective power comes from recognizing and sharing our personal myths and creating a collective women's mythology as we find our stories overlapping, interweaving, and becoming one. Collective mythology is the web that binds us all together. It helps us see the unity of our existences. Under this warm blanket of collective mythology, each of us has her own stories, her own symbols, her own dreams and values, similar though they may be to those of others.

• Share your mythology with others through telling stories and dreams, drawing images or explaining the importance of certain objects. Notice elements that are similar in different women's myths. If anyone wants to act out part of her mythology, the others can take some of the roles.

Siew Hwa Beh told the following story at a conference of four hundred people. It made the lectures on women's history and goddess mythology come alive.

I grew up in a community that prayed at the temple of Kuan Yin on the island of Pulau Pinang (Malaysia). The Goddess Kuan Yin, also known as Goddess of Mercy, is not a mediator like the Virgin Mary who stands between God and the people, nor is she Parvati, the other half of the Hindu Lord Shiva. She is the original energy and light source in the cosmos. She helps the community with their problems through oracles which are most significant when interpreted by the priestess of the Earth Goddess.

I was dedicated to her when I was two, following an oracle that saved my life. I was dying of pneumonia. An infant cousin, who caught the same illness at the same time, had passed away. It was only a matter of days before I would follow. Chinese herbal medicine could not work fast enough in this particular crisis. My mother in desperation bade my father seek an oracle from the Goddess promising a ritual dedication if my life is saved through her wisdom. After the joss-sticks of incense were offered and the bottle of oil poured to keep the flame alight, my father spoke to the Goddess. He then shook the container holding the many sticks carved with numerous inscriptions. Each stick that fell forth was confirmed or negated by the Goddess through the throwing of two halves of wood carved in the shape of a kidney. The oracle my father finally received said, "When you leave this temple you will meet a person you know. Take your problem to this person." My father was perplexed at the vagueness but did as he was advised. On leaving the temple he ran into an acquaintance. Over coffee my father presented him with the problem. He said to my father, "I just got a job as an assistant to a doctor who's recently returned from the Western world. Bring your daughter to him." Dr. Khoo pulled me through with the help of penicillin. My mother kept her word and henceforth I became the goddaughter of Kuan Yin.

My female personhood was allowed to develop outside the traditional strictures of the patriarchal society, for by saving my life the Goddess had given a sign that there was to be a higher purpose in store for me. I wandered further afield with my parents as caretakers (rather than authorities) trusting in the guidance of the Goddess. The relationship that was established between my parents and me essentially meant trusting my female psyche.

Creation Myth Meditation

Spend a few minutes relaxing. Imagine that you go on a journey to talk with the wisest, most ancient part of yourself. You may want to work with your inner guide (see chapter 2). What does this self tell you about the origins of the world? Is it different from the myths you grew up with? Record your myth. What does this myth have to tell you about the power you have to create your world?

NOTES

Here is a Hopi creation myth:

In the beginning, the earth was nothing but water. Two goddesses lived in houses on the ocean— one in the east and one in the west. The Sun on his daily passage over this new land noticed there were no living creatures there and brought this to the attention of the two deities. The goddesses were troubled. The eastern goddess visited her western counterpart to discuss the problem, making the propitious journey on a rainbow that formed a bridge.

Together, the goddesses formed a small bird of clay and brought it to life with a divine incantation. They sent the wren to fly over the newly created world in search of any living creature that might dwell there. The bird returned with the news that nothing lived in the earth and the eastern and western goddesses began to create beasts and birds of all manner, which they sent out to inhabit the world. Lastly they decided to create human beings. They molded a woman first from clay and later fashioned man. And these forms of clay were brought to life in the same manner as the beasts and birds before them.*

Mask-Making Meditation

People all over the world use masks to express different parts of their personal and collective mythology. When a woman of the Bundu masked secret society in West Africa puts on her mask, she becomes a powerful political and social figure. It is thought the Spirit works through her at that time and her judgment is respected above all. Masks have traditionally been used in sacred theater and ritual to reveal the true nature or universal spirit of a person. In a combined meditation and ritual, you can make a mask that expresses a part of your personal mythology you may not usually express.

To make an actual cast of your own face, use plaster bandages from a medical supply store. Cut them into strips about one inch wide and three inches long.

1. Put on an old shirt and pin back your hair.

2. Put vaseline on your face, or any substance that will make it easier to remove the plaster.

3. Lie down on your back.

4. Have another person wet the strips and place them on your face, leaving holes for the mouth, eyes and/or nose. Make two or three layers. Leave in place fifteen to thirty minutes, until firm enough to lift off. How does it feel to have a living mask on your face? I felt as though I had been placed in a coffin, which felt surprisingly restful and peaceful.

5. Remove, focusing on how it feels to rediscover your own face.

6. Let the mask dry overnight or longer. Make holes

---

*As reprinted and edited by Judy Chicago for The Birth Project Exhibition, Unit 3, 1983.

Woman's Mask of the Bundu, Sierra Leone, Sherbro Island; the University Museum, University of Pennsylvania, Philadelphia.

near the ears and thread ribbons through them. Tie it behind your ears to keep the mask in place.

7. Meditate on how you would like your mask to look. Paint it, apply sequins, dried flowers, and—

8. Greet yourself in a mirror.

9. Dance with your mask on.

10. Wear your mask around your house. How does it feel to be going about your everyday life with a ritual face?

11. Meet with others, acting out your masked selves.

You Are the Goddess

Talking about goddesses or the Great Goddess is difficult; consciously or unconsciously we often assume that this means "god" in a female form. The gods of patriarchal cultures reinforce the separation between the human and the divine and assume a "power-over" relationship with their followers. In contrast, goddesses—like the Earth from which they sprang—are abundantly fertile, nurturing, and include all of life in their embrace. Cultures that revere goddesses are usually more peaceful and egalitarian than god cultures.*

Using the word "goddess" may be useful as an archetype or metaphor for female energy, and the role models of goddess myths have been a powerful influence on people's lives in the past and present. In addition, talking about goddesses is a contrast to the word "god," and points out the spiritual sexism of our culture.

Ultimately, however, to be truly whole, we must recognize that there is no goddess beyond ourselves and the rest of creation. We are part of that great natural whole. It may be helpful in our movement to wholeness to refer to a female divine force, but only if we remember that it is a step in our process of reclaiming our own divinity as part of the vastness of the natural world.

---

* Elizabeth Gould Davis, *The First Sex*; Merlin Stone, *When God Was a Woman*; and *Ancient Mirrors of Womanhood*, vols. 1 and 2 (New York: New Sibylline Books, 1979).

Take, for example, the description by Siew Hwa Beh of the relationship between Kuan Yin and "worshipers":

The oracles of the Chinese goddess Kuan Yin provide guidance for those with problems, helping them anticipate (which is half the battle) or accept what cannot be changed and change what they can. The dedication to Kuan Yin does not constitute worship in the western sense, with all its reactionary and subservient connotations and paraphenalia. The temple has an open structure and is basically supported by the people who visit for oracles or meditation, paying nominal fees which are also optional. The temple is not institutionalized or affiliated with any power groups. There is really no term to describe the concept of such pollination between dedication, consultation, and psychic meditation. A word like "worship" connotes a surrendering of personal power to an authority and a mutual objectification of both. Consultation with the Goddess is of the buddhistic notion of a multi-leveled interaction, that of listening to a highly evolved ancient being or energy/light source. This source is connected to the highest potential of your own psyche on this earth plane but is even closer to it on the astral plane. This means you are truly in conference with yourself, the wisest and most ancient part of you miraculously banked as genetic memory, your own goddess in the infinite complexity of cosmic transcending spirals.

• To begin this meditation, touch different parts of your body, recognizing that the images of goddesses are made in *your* image. Name each part, saying such invocations as, "These are the breasts of the goddess, which are sensuous to touch and which nourish myself and the world"; "These are the legs of the goddess, which help me to run and dance"; "These are the eyes of the goddess, with which I see clearly all that happens." Make up your own words, sensing how you feel about yourself as the goddess. If you are with other women, take turns touching a part of the woman to your left and describe it as you would your own: "This is the hair of the goddess, which billows out, reflecting the waves of the ocean."

When you are ready to leave, say:

> "I call on the goddesses whose bodies I see
>   and feel reflected in my own body.
> I call on the goddesses whose blood, like my
>   blood, flows with the cycles of the universe.
> I call on the goddesses whose circle is never broken,
> Whose circle I am a part of wherever I go."

Living Your Reading

Books, magazines, artwork, songs, and so on are excellent sources of women's mythology (see Art Bibliography in Chapter 1 for selected sources). For later patriarchal versions of the myths, see books on mythology such as Edith Hamilton's *Greek Mythology* and the books of Joseph Campbell. For even more patriarchal versions, look around at other forms of media in our culture, such as television, movies, and advertising.

Notice ways in which patriarchal myths are often the exact opposite of their predecessors. For instance, Sheila Collins points out how women, once revered as the source of all life and nourishment, are transformed into the source of all pain and suffering, as in the patriarchal stories of Pandora (whose name literally means "all gifts") and Eve.

As you do your research, remember to "fill in the gaps" left by patriarchal researchers with your own knowledge, common sense, and intuition. Let the facts and images speak for themselves. Soon you will begin to see matrifocal influence in art and civilizations that you had not noticed before. Notice clues to older myths and obvious examples of sexism and misogyny. What do you think may have been the original myth? Notice which ones resonate for you. Why are you attracted to these stories? What does knowing about these myths do for you? What relevance do these myths have for you today? What would you like to preserve from the past? What would you like to change?

When you read about the history or see art of women in

other times and places, try imagining that the writer or artist is describing you, your family, and friends. What would it be like to live in the situations described? How would it be different from your present life? Would you perceive the world differently? If so, how? What would your emotions be like? Your thoughts? How would you relate to and use your body?

Take a few minutes every now and then to close your eyes and allow images, thoughts, and emotions to arise. You may want to write or draw your responses. Notice your dreams. They may be affected by the material, especially if you are looking at it just before you go to sleep. You may also receive more information and images from your dreams.

NOTES

5. Women as the New Healers

You are the centerfire. You are the flowering
tree.... Feel the power in yourself of woman. You
are the very mother earth itself.... Continue to use
your intuition—you can never solve a problem on the
level at which it is born.... Be the master of your
destiny, because you have the necessity to manifest
yourself.... Follow the right trail and become one
thing. Become a woman.

AGNES WHISTLING ELK
to Lynn Andrews in *Medicine Woman*

What Is Healing?

In the broadest sense, healing means making whole. Modern western medicine is based on isolating and diagnosing different parts of the body independently, rather than in relationship to one another; treating symptoms rather than causes, and overwhelming the body with drugs, artificial devices, and surgery. It tends to try to control nature, rather than working with her healing process. As a result, it is too often ineffective or destructive both physically and psychologically. Our bodies have an innate and powerful impulse towards wholeness and well-being. Natural healing (as opposed to patriarchal medicine) focuses on this impulse towards health. We are always in different states of health. Some of these have been named "sickness."

For some people, getting sick is a way to rest, receive attention, or take time to assess their lives. It's perfectly okay to be sick—and just as we can make ourselves sick, each of us has the power to make herself well and to stay well. Although stressful living conditions are sometimes unavoidable, you can affect your health enormously by how you respond to these conditions and how you structure your life and attitudes.

Healing is part of the body's natural cycle. If we allow the body and the healing information we get through meditation to guide us, we can reclaim much of our healing power. Receiving help from friends and professionals may also be an important aspect of our healing power—as long as we remember that each of us is the ultimate authority for her own health.

Natural healing is a way of living fully and consciously with an understanding of the natural cycles of perpetual change and renewal. It may employ herbs and nutrition, meditation, acupuncture, various forms of massage or any number of other methods to treat the whole person—her mind, emotions, and spirit, as well as her body—so that her maximum potential for well-being can be tapped. Anything we do to facilitate the flow of energy between different parts of ourselves and between ourselves and others is healing.

Some people associate the energy we use to maintain or regain health with electromagnetic currents and the workings of the autonomic nervous system. In Chinese and Japanese, it is called *chi* or *ki* and is regarded as the life-force of the universe. Acupuncture and herbal medicine work with it, and physical and spiritual disciplines such as t'ai chi and aikido attempt to tap its power. I use this concept of vital forces to apply to health. Working with this force can be an extremely powerful meditation, and the usual separation between healer and healed is broken down.

Women and Healing

Women hold the keys to much of natural healing. As we heal ourselves, we reclaim the powers that women possessed throughout most of history. It is significant that women predominate in the modern holistic health movement, whereas male MDs far outnumber females. Natural healing is more accessible to women and more appealing to many.

In Paleolithic and Neolithic societies, it is likely that most of the healers were women. Women seemed to have a magical connection with the forces of life. They could create human beings from their own bodies, and their bodies produced food for the newborn. Women learned how to work with nature and the changes in their own bodies.

In preagricultural societies, women were generally the breadwinners; their gathering provided most of the food for their communities. Gradually, in their gathering activities, women discovered healing herbs and mind-altering plants—and invented agriculture. They applied to healing the lessons of natural cycles they learned from their own experiences of plants and seasons, menstruation, pregnancy, and child-rearing. They became healers because they knew how to work *with* nature. They learned how to tap psychic powers as well as physical ones.

Women's power as healers, like women's power in all areas of life, waned as the patriarchy gained in strength. In their book *Witches, Midwives, and Nurses,** Barbara Ehrenreich and Deidre English trace the decline of natural healing practices in the West over the centuries, as the developing medical profession—Christian and male-dominated—set out to eradicate its competitors and the "pagan" nature religions with which natural healing was associated. Millions of natural healers were burned as witches. The majority of these were women.****

Women have continued to work as herbalists, psychics, and midwives, but they have been persecuted and denigrat-

*Barbara Ehrenreich and Deidre English, *Witches, Midwives, and Nurses* (New York: The Feminist Press, 1973).

**The battle against natural healing practices persists to this day, especially as the upsurge of natural healing threatens the medical establishment. Successful midwives, foot reflexologists, herbalists, and homeopaths—both women and men—have been arrested as their healing powers become more potent. Standards do need to be set for quality in healing, and this can only happen when natural healing is recognized and legalized.

ed. Women make up 70 percent of the American medical profession, mostly as nurses, aides, and maintenance workers, with little controlling power. Only 13 percent of American doctors are women.* At the same time, sexist gynecological "care," advertising, and male violence oppress us through our bodies.

Small wonder that one of the first areas the feminist movement focused on was women's health care! Feminists set up women's health centers, fought for abortion rights, and started researching and practicing natural healing methods, synthesizing ancient knowledge with what we want to retain of modern medicine and creating new healing techniques.

As we reclaim our healing powers, we reclaim power in all parts of our lives. We literally take our lives and bodies into our own hands. We assert our right to be whole and healthy people—both psychologically and physically. We begin to reclaim a tremendous amount of money and power from the medical industry. In the process, we gain a wider and deeper wisdom.

I personally experienced this transformation in 1973 when I healed myself of cervical dysplasia, a "precancerous" condition, and amenorrhea (absence of menses). I was terrified—and determined to heal myself, though I had had no such experience and knew no one else who had. I used the few tools I knew at the time: I went on a yoga retreat, which consisted of ten days of fasting, silence, yoga, and meditation, for I felt that I needed some drastic measures to get back in touch with my body. In my everyday life, I ate a strict health food diet and drank herbal teas. I also went once to a healer who used the ancient technique of laying on of hands. Within two months, the dysplasia was gone and my menses returned for the first time in one-and-a-half years.

_____

*Bureau of Statistics, U.S. Department of Labor, 1980.

My gynecologist was shocked, and made fun of my techniques. I didn't care—not only was I not going to die or have a hysterectomy in ten years, as my doctor had implied, but I had healed myself! Everything that I had been teaching about natural healing and the power of women reclaiming our bodies was true! Later, I met many women with stories similar to mine. We all felt that our self-healing had been a turning point in our lives, and that the empowerment we felt in healing our own bodies was as important as the physical healing.

Healing with the Hands

An important tool I used in my self-healing was tapping the healing energy in the hands. Laying on of hands, or "bodywork," takes many forms, including shiatsu, massage, polarity therapy, and acupressure. All bodywork assumes that the body, mind, and emotions are integrally related through one energy. Women have been encouraged to use touch, much more so than men, and a look at any listing of body workers will show that women predominate in using this facility for healing.

We can learn to feel this energy in our own and others' bodies and direct its flow to heal ourselves physically and psychologically. The pathways along which this energy travels sometimes correspond to muscles, nerves, and bones. Blockages in the energy flow are caused by, and result in, physical, mental, and emotional distress. By applying pressure with the hands to certain particularly sensitive points along the energy pathways, we can release the energy where it is blocked or draw it to places where it is not flowing. The release of energy may be felt immediately as relaxation, tingling, warmth, or inner peace, and, in the long run, as cure and prevention of sickness.

Laying on of hands is one of the most important aspects of womanspirit. When we use touch, one of our least developed senses, we rediscover the closeness of our bodies and our spirits. We experience, and create firsthand what is "holy"—*whole*, in the true sense.

My first experience in healing came when one of the women in my women's group could barely make to our regular meeting. She had had an experimental IUD for several months and had started bleeding heavily the day before. She was so weak she had had to leave work. I didn't know if I could help her, but I had recently learned in a polarity therapy workshop how to use the deep, gentle pressure of my hands to relieve menstrual cramps. I did what I knew: applied pressure to the appropriate points on her back in rhythm with the flow of her breath, occasionally asking her to direct her breath to the points I was working on. The next morning she was hardly bleeding at all, and I worked on her again for an hour. The bleeding stopped soon after that. I was surprised and even felt awe. Yet hadn't I learned these techniques so I could heal myself and others?

Months later, my roommate had her IUD taken out. She began hemorrhaging heavily, with clots the size of her finger. This went on for twenty-four hours. Then I tried the same combination of breath awareness and pressure points I had used before. Once again the bleeding completely stopped—this time immediately.

I knew that the exchange of energy between these women and me was crucial to the healing. I felt affirmed in my ability to do something for them myself, instead of just offering my condolences or taking them to a hospital. Most of all, it worked! I realized that I had discovered a powerful tool as well as a great responsibility. I knew that others could discover their own healing abilities as easily as I had.

As I continued to do bodywork on other people, I found I often went into a very pleasurable and sometimes intense state of meditation unlike any other I had experienced. I became aware of my body as a flow of energy. I felt the atoms revolving, my organs working, and my blood flowing. I felt my body as a reflection of everything going on in the rest of the universe. It was clear that working with the body in this way not only had political implications in the tool it gave us for healing ourselves, but also was a very "spiritual" experience. The lines between the "spiritual" and the "political" began to break down for me.

Giving and receiving bodywork has become an essential part of my life—in maintaining my own physical and emotional well-being, in healing other people, as a chance to be with friends in a deep way, and as a source of great pleasure. The depth of the experience is usually intensified when I am working in a group and when I have a close relationship with the other person or people. Any meditation, ritual, meeting, or class goes better and is far more meaningful if we do bodywork as a part of it. Opening up the physical channels allows the mental and emotional experience to reverberate throughout our whole beings, as every cell becomes receptive to it.

Energy Meditation

Here is a meditation you can do to help you feel this energy and direct it through your hands. You can also work with someone else, taking turns leading each other through the exercise.

• Find some time and a place where you can be quiet for at least half an hour. If you wear clothing make sure it's comfortable. Sit down cross-legged on the floor or in a chair with your feet on the floor. Feel what your body is experiencing. Shift around until you find a good, balanced position. The "best" position for bodywork is the one that feels the most comfortable to you. If you feel strained or uncomfortable, this will cut off your energy.

• Rub your hands together quickly for several seconds and then stop and see how they feel. Now raise your hands so that they are in front of your belly, palms facing one another, a few inches apart. Close your eyes and notice where your breathing is and what it is like. Don't try to change it; just observe it for a while. If your breath wants to change itself, let it.

• After awhile, imagine that as you exhale, you send your breath across your shoulders and down each arm, and that the air comes out a hole in the middle of each palm. What would it feel like if you actually could send your breath down through your arms and hands? What sensations do you have?

• When you have spent several minutes doing this, you can begin to play around with the feeling between your hands. You can move your hands apart and together, in time with your breathing. If you feel that they want to make a shape in the air, let them.

• With your hands, touch your face, your neck, your arms, your torso, your legs—all the while feeling the energy and life that are within you. If a part of your body needs healing, spend a longer time with your hands resting on that part, feeling your breath receiving and giving out energy through your hands. Remember that healing means making whole.

• Go to a plant or an animal and move your hands slowly toward it, feeling its energy. Finally, massage your feet. The feet exchange energy with the earth. Take some time to see how you feel now and assimilate the energy.

I always feel revitalized after working on myself in this way. Hunger, speediness, tightness, and exhaustion can vanish.

NOTES

Guidelines

As you learn to feel the energy in another person's body, you can connect her energy with yours and draw this connected energy through her body, so that both of your energies are replenished and more evenly distributed.

Here are some key points to keep in mind when working on another person:

• First, be sure that you are comfortable. You may feel some awkwardness when you are first experimenting, but stop before it gets to be too much. If you are tense, either physically (from not sitting easily or freely) or mentally (from trying too hard to do it "right"), your energy will not be flowing as well and you won't be able to heal as well or to enjoy yourself. Don't overextend yourself. Women have been giving for centuries. Sometimes we don't know when to stop giving or how to receive. Trying to heal someone when you are exhausted, sick, upset, or have mixed feelings about doing the bodywork (for whatever reason) is not good for either of you. However, if you are feeling good, or only mildly tired or scattered, doing bodywork on someone will probably energize and center you.

• Use your sensitivity to feel the energy in your own body and hands and in the body of the other person to judge whether a light or heavy pressure is appropriate, when to gradually increase or decrease the pressure, when to go on to another point, and when to end the bodywork session. You want to touch in a way that allows contact and release (which can be felt as "good pain"), but that doesn't cause a person to tense up ("bad pain"). Watch your partner's breathing and body changes. Trust your sense of timing about how long to maintain contact. There is a point at which a person has released all she is going to for that particular session; extra time would be wasted or draining to both of you. Different people and situations require different approaches. Sometimes you may feel it's appropriate to spend half an hour simply holding someone's head.

• Use both hands, even when one hand is only resting lightly on the other person's body. This keeps the energy current flowing between you.

• In general, work on only one point at a time. Pressure applied to more than one place is usually too much for a person to respond to. There are some exceptions—as when you are working on the head, or when you are drawing the energy between two places.

• Communicate with the other person, both during and after a bodywork session. Ask her what different points feel like, if she would like more or less pressure. Ask her to communicate anything she wants even when you don't ask. Tell her what you feel happening. You may want to be silent or make sounds on exhaling breaths.

• Doing bodywork may give rise to emotions and images that show a long-forgotten association with the part of the body that is being worked on. If the memory is an unpleasant one, you can bring it out into the open and discuss it. If it is positive, you can build upon it and develop it. You don't have to talk the whole time, but communicating with each other as you go along helps as a focus.

• After you have worked on a person and she has had a chance to rest, ask her how she feels. Then ask her to walk around, feeling the ground beneath her. Ask if she is walking differently, if things look the same as before, and how her mental state is.

• Ground the energy. Since you have been merging with someone else's energy, you want to make sure there is a clear separation between the two of you when the session is over. You can do this during the session by allowing the energy to flow through you, as if it were water and you were a channel. If you need to, after working on someone, touch your hands to the earth to let out the excess energy or hold your hands under water. You can also mentally tell yourself three things that are different about you and the other person (e.g., her hair is red, yours is black, and so on).

• Work with the outcome. People sometimes feel worse before they feel better. Discharging pent-up energy and built-up toxins is a necessary part of the healing process. If the person you have worked on feels no better, or feels worse, question why. Does she need more work? Was she resisting? Were you too tired, disinterested, or otherwise not connecting with her? Does she need additional forms of healing? Natural healing is based on a holistic approach, encompassing many forms of healing. Sometimes, acupuncture or western medicine can provide the best treatment for an individual at a particular time in her life. Consider including other forms of healing, in addition to your own, for complicated situations.

• Practice! Learn from others, learn from your own experience and intuition, and learn from being "wrong." The more you work at it, the more you'll get the hang of it. You will adapt techniques you have learned from others to fit your own needs and the needs of different people you work with. As you are experiencing yourself as a channel, remember that you are responsible for enabling yourself to tap this energy. The more you acknowledge what you do, the more you will be able to learn from yourself.

The Head and Belly Circle

This exercise will help you learn to feel another person's energy. It is also a simple but effective way to balance the energy between two people at the beginning or end of body-work session. You can use it to heal someone of headaches, stomach pains, general tension, or lethargy. You can also do it on yourself.

To both of you: Find a place where you and a friend can be quiet for at least half an hour. This will give you time to take turns working on each other and to assimilate some of the energy when you are finished. Make sure your clothing is loose and comfortable. One of you lies down on her back and the other sits on her friend's right side, so that she can comfortably reach the forehead and belly of her friend.

To the person lying down: Find a way that you can rest comfortably on the floor with your arms and legs uncrossed, so that your body is free and relaxed. If your back hurts, you can bend your knees or put a pillow under them. Do you feel as though you are in contact with the floor in some places more than in others? Where in your body do you feel your breathing? What is its pace? Don't try to breathe a special way, just allow your breathing to find its own rhythm. After you have given attention to how you are lying, simply stay aware of your being and any changes you feel.

To the person sitting: Make sure that you are sitting so that you can comfortably reach your friend. Bring your hands into the air in front of your belly, so that the palms are facing one another and a few inches apart. Close your eyes and notice how your hands feel. As in the first exercise in this chapter, start imagining that as you exhale you send your breath across your shoulders and down each arm, and that the air comes out a hole in the middle of each palm. What sensations do you have? When you have spent several minutes doing this, begin to play around with the feeling between your hands. Move your hands apart and together as you inhale and exhale. Trace the outline of the energy with your hands. Move your hands along the outline of the energy.

• When you are ready, gently bring one hand to rest on your friend's forehead and the other to rest on her belly. Continue imagining that your breath and energy are traveling along your arms, but now feel that when you exhale you send your breath-energy down the arm that connects with your friend's belly, out that hand, and into her belly. Your energy mingles with her energy, smoothing out and releasing any blockages there. It travels up her torso, along her spine, through her neck and head into your other hand, where you receive it as you inhale. Then it moves up that arm and across

your shoulders, to be exhaled out the other arm and hand into your friend's belly—and so on around, continuing the cycle and creating an unbroken circuit of energy.

• Are you experiencing any emotions, colors, images, memories, or physical sensations? Ask your friend if she is.

• Continue this breath-energy circle until you feel that the energy is complete, or for as long as you feel comfortable. If you feel that other parts of your friend would like some contact, touch or hold them, all the while thinking energy. Be sure not to do so much that either of you gets tired. Finally, spend a minute touching her head and belly and make up a prayer, affirmation, or wish for both of you.

• When you are finished, if any parts of yourself would like some energy, touch them as well, bringing your energy back to yourself.

• To both of you: How do you feel now, compared with when you started? How is your body? Your emotional state? Your thoughts? What is the energy in the room like? Although this is a very simple exercise, people's reactions to it are usually profound. When you are ready, you can share with one another what you experienced, then switch places and start over again.

I find the head and belly circle extraordinarily peaceful and energizing, whether I am working on someone else, or she on me. Whatever has been running around the surface of my mind falls away, as well as the blockages in my body's electrical currents and in my muscles. Working on another person starts on the "physical" level; soon my mind, my whole being, has gone through a radical transformation. Images, emotions, memories, dreams, visions, and realizations float up through my consciousness. I feel in a state of complete equilibrium, close to my source. Here are some other women's reactions:

"Your hands felt cold at first, but then they got really warm. I could actually feel the energy shooting up my spine to my head. I've never felt that before."

"I've had menstrual cramps all day, but your hand on my belly was so gentle that now I can hardly feel them."

"I feel great from having worked on you! I was really tired when I came in. It's as though you *gave* me energy."

• You can also "draw energy" between other parts of the body. Have your friend lie down and relax, taking a few deep breaths. Hold or touch two places on her body where bones are prominent. Pay particular attention to joints—of arms and legs, vertebrae, pelvis, bones. Energy flows most freely along them. Allow your breath and energy to flow between these two places, just as you did in the head and belly circle. Move your hands to new places or remove them entirely as your intuition guides you.

Pressure Points for Women

After focusing yourself and the other person through an exercise such as the head and belly circle, you can work on specific points, such as these buttock points, which are especially good for any kind of pelvic blockage or tension, such as lower back pain and menstrual cramps.

One person lies down on her back, stomach, or side. The other sits to one side, where she can comfortably reach her friend's buttocks.

To the person sitting: Many points on the buttocks are sensitive. One in particular is very powerful. It is located in the lower middle of the buttock. To find it, press in on your own or your friend's buttock. You may have to press hard at first, but once you find it, press in just enough to make contact. Place the other hand on your friend's hipbone or tailbone. Hold the point until you feel some release, see a change in her breathing, feel energy, or intuit that it is time to move on. Explore to find other sensitive points on the buttocks. Don't forget to do both sides.

Apply gentle pressure to sensitive points near bones, such as the sacrum, tailbone, hipbone, and lower spine. Be sure not to press in (towards the center of the body) on bones.

End with the head and belly circle.

Group Healing

Using healing energy in a group is an extremely powerful meditation and creates strong community bonds. The recipient feels the full focus of the group and, since the energy flows throughout the circle, everyone is healed. Group healing meditations are especially important for women, since we usually have a hard time receiving attention. This issue was pointed out by a woman who had cancer and who came to one of my groups. Her friends had done a healing ritual for her that she described to the group. The part I remember most vividly is their chant: "If we give it to you, will you take it?"

Channeling Energy

One person lies down on her back in the middle of the

circle with her arms and legs uncrossed. The others gather around her, each touching her at a different place so that someone is touching every point of her body that seems to need attention.

To the person lying down: Allow your body to settle into the floor. Feel each part—back, legs, arms, head. Breathe into them. Ask yourself if you want to receive this energy from your friends. If you feel embarrassed or have any other initial reactions, say them. Then let go of your self-consciousness.

To the circle: Close your eyes and get in touch with your own breath-energy and your own stillness. Feel yourself as part of the circle and part of the person you are touching. Direct your breath-energy through your hands, so that it travels through the person you are touching, into all the other members, through the circle, and back to you. Visualize, feel, and know that with each breath you are helping heal the person in the middle of the circle and that she is healing herself. Imagine that every time your heart beats, old cells are being cleaned out of her body and your bodies and new healthy ones being created. Imagine the fresh blood flowing throughout her. The more it flows, the more old cells die and new ones are born. Imagine all the wastes being cleaned out. Affirm to yourself that all of you and she have fresh, strong, healthy bodies and that you and she will continue in good health.

You may feel at times that there is too much congested energy and that you would like to brush or wipe it away. Simply brush your hands lightly over the person or let go of her and shake your hands.

Be sensitive to the energy of the group. When you feel ready to end, pass your hands over the person lying in the middle of the circle, either dusting her off or passing your hands in the air just above her.

If there are enough of you (it doesn't take many people), you can lift the person you are healing. Gently slip your hands under the person lying down. Be sure that someone is holding her head. Hold her for awhile. Then slowly lift her into the air—above your shoulders, if you can. When she is lifted, gently rock her. You can chant her name or a song. Then gently lower her to the ground. Pass your hands over her and end by holding her feet for a few moments.

Distance Healing

This is a variation on the basic energy circle, the circle of hands, and on the exercise for healing someone actually in the circle.

• Decide on a person not present whom you want to receive healing energy. Let everyone know her name and some description of her. If you want someone to verbally direct this healing, decide who will do it.

• Sit in a circle holding hands. Send your breath-energy around the circle of hands as described above. Direct your attention to the person who is to receive the energy. Imagine that the energy is flowing out of your circle straight to her. Visualize, feel, and know that with each breath you are helping heal the absent person and that she is healing herself. Continue to imagine her cells, blood, and breath being cleansed and revitalized. Feel the healing energy pouring back into the circle and into you, so that everyone is healed.

• When you are ready to end, gradually withdraw your energy from the person to whom you have been sending it by bringing your attention back to the place where you are sitting, the circle, and yourself. Focus on the breath in your belly or notice three things that are different between you and the person to whom you were sending energy (e.g., you are forty; she is twenty-three, and so on). Gradually bring your attention to the energy flowing around the circle and become more aware of your own body. Feel your blood as it courses through your body, carrying away old cells and helping create new ones. Affirm to yourself that you are healthy in mind, body, and spirit. Feel the totality of your energy. When you are ready, let go of your neighbors' hands. Touch yourself, your hands now energized from the circle.

Tell one another what you experienced, draw it, or write it.

Self-Healing

Using the same focused energy as in Distance Healing, you can heal yourself by "imagining" it. Visualize a healing color around the sick part of yourself. You can imagine a rainbow passing through you, your body absorbing only those colors that would be beneficial to you. Feel how you would feel energetic and healthy. Breathe deeply, taking in health and clarity with each inhalation, and releasing sickness and blocked energy with each exhalation.

Here is a description by Margo Adair, teacher of Applied Meditation, of how she heals herself.

I used to have a runny nose all winter long. It had never occurred to me before to imagine my mucous membranes drying up until I started doing healing meditations. In a couple of days the problem was gone and has never reoccurred! I used to be sick an average of ten days a year and for the past six years I haven't been sick for more than one day a year. I used to believe that when I got sick I was supposed to go to bed and wait for my ailment to disappear of its own accord. Now I know better. I know I can go inside myself, understand my ailment by imagining talking to it, thus gaining insights which enable me to know where I need to make changes in my life so I don't cause it again. I also imagine it healing; this process facilitates a much quicker return to health. Now, if I get the flu I have it for only one day instead of a week.

In a similar way, you can use the power of your imagination to protect yourself in traumatic situations. According to Margo:

Three years after I began meditating I had a profound experience that revealed to me the degree to which I had come to know the power of the body/mind and how much I had *regained* my power. I was moving a refrigerator on a dolly, pulling it backwards down a driveway into the street. The driveway, rather than the gradual decline I had expected, moved from sidewalk level to street level very quickly. All of a sudden the refrigerator was pushing me—I wasn't pulling it—and then I tripped on a four-by-four board. As I fell, I *instantly* imagined drawing in healing energies to protect myself. Under "normal" material conditions (whatever they are) the leverage created by the bars of the dolly and the corner of the four-by-four was such that the bones of my legs would have snapped under the impact of the refrigerator. If I had responded with fear, expecting to hurt myself, my body would have responded by receiving the full impact and my legs would have been crushed. Instead, when I landed on the pavement I felt this incredible mushroom of energy holding up the refrigerator. Afterwards my legs didn't hurt and that energy continued to buzz through me for the rest of the move we were making that day—almost as if I'd taken a psychedelic.*

Creativity and Healing

Using our creativity is a powerful component in healing ourselves. Here is a description by Mary Hope Lee, a poet and dollmaker, of how she used her art to help heal herself after an abortion:

Valentine's Day 1978, four days before my 31st birthday, I had an abortion. It was a most difficult decision, a truly heavy burden to bear. My hope was that I was acting as a vehicle for some highly evolved soul whose only need was for a brief moment in the flesh so that it might spin free of the karmic wheel. Having been raised a Catholic—although no longer practicing that religion—made the burden of the abortion all the more heavy. It restricted my life, stifled my sexuality, worried me incessantly. I needed a way to transform what troubled me, to release it, to prune the dead flower all the way back to the root, to stop its ceaseless leeching of joy from my heart.

I thought perhaps if I bought a doll to represent the spirit of the aborted one I would be able to acknowledge its influence in and on my life in a more constructive way. The gesture was unsatisfactory,

---

*Margo Adair, *Working Inside Out: Tools for Change*, work-in-progress.

incomplete. There was no resolution. I found the solution, instead, in my own dollmaking. To make a doll whose source was from within me where the struggle raged was the only way. Thus was born Winter Valentine, a little being with large saucer eyes, an exposed heart, arms raised on high. Now she sits with Baron Samedi in his flamboyant feathered hat, a *Loa* [diety] of the Haitian Vodoun pantheon, harbinger of that transformation we call death and with Oyá, her heart-shaped amethyst third eye flashing, a Yoruba goddess of Nigeria West Africa, who watches over the welfare of departed souls and their earthly abodes in graveyards and cemeteries.

A woman who did not know their story commented to me, while looking at this little trio of beings, that they all seemed so joyous to her. Joyous, yes! Death is at last transformed, burden is lifted, guilt and shame and regret released and resolved.*

Herbs

Herbs have been used for thousands of years as food and as medicine. The popular image of the witch with her house

*From private communication with the author, 1983.

full of herbs is a historical memory of times when natural healing prevailed and women were the healers.

The healing properties of most herbs can easily be extracted by drinking teas made from them or by using them in cooking. There are several good books on herbs and their healing powers. You can look up herbs for your specific needs and experiment with them. Respect their powers: like many medicines, some herbs can be harmful in large doses.

• My favorite herbal tea is Womanspirit tea, which I serve in all my groups. Here's the recipe: Put one teaspoon of licorice root and a cinnamon stick in a quart of water. Bring to a boil. If you want a sweeter tea, you can simmer it for up to fifteen minutes. Take the kettle off the fire, and add one teaspoon each of peppermint, lemon grass, and another tea whose taste will blend with the others. I usually add a tea known for its powerful healing properties, like comfrey or alfalfa. Steep for three to five minutes. Drink!

• My favorite powerful food healer is garlic. Ounce for ounce, garlic is said to be more powerful than penicillin. It has been used as a cure-all for thousands of years and is still used in many countries today. Whenever I wake up with a sore throat or stuffy nose, I chop up a garlic clove and put it in the blender with a glass of orange juice. The garlic taste is hardly noticeable. If I need to, I have another later on in the day and in the evening. Almost every time, the cold is gone by the next morning. If not, I take more garlic. As a result, I have had only one or two colds in the last decade. Like all healing treatments, it works most effectively if I take it as soon as possible.

Taking remedies provides a good opportunity to visualize healing taking place as described in the self-healing meditation. The healing effect will be strengthened incredibly, no matter what medicine you are taking, if you focus on the act and let awareness of your health and well-being fill your mind, remembering that you have the power to heal yourself.

6. Creating New Rituals

> Rituals, especially the rituals of the sacred circle—
> the hoop of life which contains all things—remind us
> that we all spring from the center, the source, the
> All-That-Is; that the aliveness of the Great Spirit lives
> in each of us; and that we all have an equal place in
> things. In remembering, we can again become mem-
> bers of the Great Family. The four-legged, wingeds,
> the rock people and green growing ones are inviting
> us now to awaken and step again with love fully into
> that great circle. Let us find good relationship with
> all things in a daily ritual—be it inner, outer, silent,
> or sung—for *all* our relatives. Ho!
>
> BROOKE MEDICINE EAGLE

There are times when inner meditation or quiet spiritual
work is more restricting than beneficial. It is important not
to confuse legitimate discipline with making yourself miser-
able. When quiet work doesn't seem to be appropriate, you
can turn it into play by combining the various techniques
described in earlier chapters with movement, sound, and
physical objects. Pageantry and symbolic action have been a
part of all formal spiritual endeavors, but many traditional
rituals have become repetitive and empty. Creating your
own rituals to meet immediate needs and using your personal material can make rituals come alive and remind us
why they were used in the first place. If you are working
with a group, you will also find that doing rituals together
can be an important way to focus concentration, create a
special positive atmosphere, and deepen your bonds.

Rituals have been common throughout human existence.
Mythology, archaeology, linguistics, art, and history tell us
of the rituals that our foremothers performed. Paleolithic
caves as wombs of the earth mother seem natural sites for

birth and rebirth rituals, and the carved and painted breasts and vulvas, paintings of animals and plants, and markings of the cycles of the moon and seasons still preserved in some of these caves are vivid reminders of ancient spirituality.

Right up until the classical period, the most powerful and important religious experience in ancient Greek culture was the Eleusian mysteries, believed to have been founded by the earth goddess Demeter to celebrate her reunion with her daughter Persephone/Kore. The mysteries were brilliantly designed to facilitate a psychic rebirth in the participant that corresponded to Persephone/Kore's return from the underworld and the re-emergence of spring.

In the past, ritual was a comprehensive, holistic celebration and expression of human creativity and cyclic regeneration. Many of our arts—theater, poetry, and song—originally evolved as parts of one ritual-making process. The participants in ancient rituals often had an active part in the ceremony—as they do in many contemporary traditional cultures.

Ritual is an integral and essential part of human existence. We treasure both old and new repeated rituals because they give us a sense of our own continuity. They allow us time and space for a perspective on the rest of our lives. However, in more technologically advanced countries, rituals have been so institutionalized and co-opted by authority figures (who are rarely women) that any spontaneous or original rituals are suspect and lack authority. In addition, the rituals we do have often consist of meaningless repeated action removed from the original context and feelings. Ritual is too often used to maintain the status quo and the result is alienation, fear, and reinforcement of hierarchy.

Patriarchal ritual, in the form of many traditional religious services and patriotic holidays, is relatively dead as a spiritual experience. It is cut off from two essential aspects of ritual—spontaneous creative psychic power, and the cycles of nature. We feel this emptiness in our lives and so create rituals of our own— often without recognizing them as such. Support group meetings, sports, parties, eating, and playing together often become rituals. The unofficial nature of such festivities allows them to remain fluid and vital. However, they do not usually have the power and effectiveness of a focused and purposeful ritual.

We need to create celebrations that are alive and that are relevant to our needs as twentieth-century women. Many people feel self-conscious at the idea of creating new rituals. However, a ritual that is used as a personal or group meditation can be immensely powerful and vital. Rituals drawn from our present lives and memories can give us a sense of our personal and collective history and development. Rituals can be spontaneous or planned, and can be used daily or for special events. They are wonderful for celebrations, for new beginnings, and for cycles of the months and years. The cycles of the seasons were an integral part of traditional ritual, for they helped us understand and make use of our own corresponding seasonal and lifetime fluctuations.

Two basic theories explain how ritual works: the psychic view (ritual works with the unseen and seen forces of the universe to affect material reality), and the psychological view (ritual affects people's actions by affecting their minds). They are essentially one and the same. The psychological approach also acknowledges the political, economic, and social realms, and emphasizes our total power, rather than our helplessness, by offering concrete, effective tools for changing our old patterns. The psychic approach to ritual recognizes and uses the interrelationship of humans, animals, plants, and electromagnetic and geophysical forces to become a truly holistic science. By tapping and using *all* powers, we can learn to live sanely and healthfully on this planet.

Personal Rituals

Rituals fall into several general categories that often overlap: spontaneous and planned, personal and collective, and repeated and occasional. Energy applied towards any one ritual will carry over into other areas of your life.

Perhaps even more so than with other Womanspirit work, the ultimate purpose of ritual is to learn to spontaneously create your own, according to the needs of the time and place. For this reason, in this chapter I am giving more examples of rituals than directions.

Recognizing Your Daily Personal Rituals

You already perform many daily rituals. The way you dress, get ready for work, eat, accomplish tasks, and relax can be rituals, although you may not have thought of them as rituals before. Some of these may be "mindless" rituals that literally put your rational mind to rest so that your more meditative mind can emerge. Recognizing them as ritual can give you a larger sense of your capacity for experience. This recognition can also allow you to become more aware of your actions, just as Zen Buddhism encourages people to perform the most mundane actions as consciously as possible. Other rituals you do may be automatic routines that keep you from experiencing life more fully. These you may want to focus on and change, as in the following exercises.

Many of our "negative" rituals are known as "bad habits" —such as smoking, drinking or eating too much, or other compulsive behavior and substance abuse. Do you have any negative rituals? Most of us do. Consider transforming them into positive rituals. Here are some examples:

One of my occasional negative rituals is eating too hastily and more than I need. I made up a positive eating ritual for myself. Before eating, I sit for a minute or two centering myself and focusing on exchanging energy with the food. If I am with others, we often hold hands before we eat. I eat less nervously now, get more energy from less food, and have more respect for the food itself and for the animals, plants, and people who produced it. I also enjoy eating much more than I did before.

Another negative ritual I have is overreacting with hurt, fear, or confusion to certain situations. I began a ritual of breathing deeply whenever I caught myself beginning to overreact. (The key here, as in most rituals, is recognizing the negative energy when it arises, rather than after it is well underway.) If I have to act immediately in a situation, I do so, trying to feel my energy emanating from the center of my body.

If I have more time, I breathe into my belly and focus on what is bothering me. As my immediate reactions die down, the underlying internal cause of my overreaction emerges. By tuning into what is really going on, I find out information about myself, other people, and the situation that otherwise would be obscured by my overreaction. I can deal with the situation better, as well as identify and change the part of myself that overreacts. I feel power replace my anxiety. I decide how I want to use that power. Sometimes I do a ritual to focus or symbolize the new direction of my energy, so that I can more easily carry it over into the rest of my life.

Creating New Rituals

Every ritual is different, and the most important rule is to create a structure in which you can be spontaneous. The power of ritual comes from the fact that we create it ourselves. I can give you some general guidelines. You do the rest.

The three main steps of a personal ritual are: (1) *focusing* on your purpose and preparing yourself for it; (2) *clearing* out any internal and external forces blocking you from it; and (3) *transforming* your previously inhibited energy into constructive energy that will help you attain your goal.

Decide on your purpose. You can do a ritual to help someone get well, protect your house, attain success in your work—anything that you are doing something about on the material plane. (Always ask permission before you do a ritual that will affect someone else.) You may want to choose an object that symbolizes your purpose and include it in your ritual as a talisman that will become charged with your energy.

When you are making up a ritual, draw on sources from all aspects of your life: meditations, dreams, exercises, childhood games, research, group inspiration, fantasies, and so on. I first got the idea for the cord ritual I describe here in a meditation in which I "saw" a thread weaving in and out of a circle of women. I had taken part in Tibetan rituals in which each person receives a piece of cloth blessed by a lama-priest for good luck. It was clear that the power of our circle was so strong that our cord was already blessed as our own birth cord, which we could divide among us, each keeping a piece. Another inspiration for a ritual came in a dream in which I saw a group of women dancing, each with a strip of cloth in her hand, which extended her energy in a flowing movement. I used this idea for a ritual for five hundred people. It worked beautifully.

Here are some other examples of the kind of symbolic action you can do as rituals. Use your imagination to create others.

Candle ritual: Choose a special candle for its shape, size, and color. Prepare a safe place to burn it. You may want to cover the area with tin foil. During your ritual meditation, write on the candle with a sharp instrument some symbols or words that relate to the intended outcome of the ritual. Imagine that you are pouring all your energy into the candle. Light the candle and meditate for a few minutes on your purpose. Feel that, as the candle burns, negative energy is disappearing and positive creative energy is being released into the universe and inside of you. Leave the candle burning until it goes out by itself while you go about your life. As it burns down, the light will accomplish your purpose. If you must leave your house, or want to do a longer spell, you can repeat the ritual every day, burning only part of the candle. Take care to prevent a fire.

Cord ritual: Take a piece of string, ribbon, or cloth. In

your meditation, tie a certain number of knots in it. Each time you tie a knot, make an affirmation about the outcome of your ritual. Make it as strong and immediate as possible: "_____ is happening right now," rather than, "I wish it would happen" or "It will happen in a while." When you finish the ritual, leave the cord knotted. Meditate once a day, touching one knot at a time and repeating your affirmation. When you feel like you have meditated on the subject enough, untie each knot, saying, "It is done ... it is done." You can then save the cord for a special purpose, or burn it.

Here is one way to create your own ritual:

• Choose a time (allow about half an hour to an hour) and place where you can be undisturbed. Do not do rituals when you are feeling too scattered or tired. Make this a pleasant experience for yourself. This is an opportunity to create a peaceful, beautiful, and focused space in your life. Affirm your power to do this. Decide what tools you will use: candles, incense, flowers, symbolic or powerful objects, musical instruments.

• Sit and center yourself through deep breathing or other bodywork. Use one of the inner meditation skills (e.g., guidework, dreamwork) to focus on what is blocking you from your goal, both externally and internally. Examine all aspects of the situation without judgment. Meditate on how you can change the energy. What do you need to do internally? Externally?

• Visualize an image or find a word, sensation, or other symbol that represents the energy you want to change.

• See it transforming until it symbolizes the outcome you want. Dance or use your own special movements, sing, direct your attention to a symbolic object, draw, or use other actions (like the candle or cord ritual) to channel creative energy toward your goal and to represent its fulfillment. Celebrate your own power to change your life!

• Bring the ritual to a close. Ground the energy through deep breathing or other bodywork.

I have a special table set up in my room that I use for

meditating and for rituals. Its appearance changes as I change. Here's what I do in an "average" ritual:

I arrange whatever tools I am going to use, and stretch or breathe deeply to loosen myself up. Then I light candles and incense to add warmth and light and the element of fire. They help focus my energy. I may walk around the room with the incense to clear it out and to call on the new forces I want to enter. I like the smell of the incense and the way the smoke moves.

I sit in front of my table and spend a few minutes focusing on my breathing. Then I ring my Tibetan chimes, calling on the spirits within me and without me to attend to this ritual. If I have any special objects to be "charged" or that feel related to the ritual, I put them on the table. I do a form of guided meditation and "go inside" and talk to whatever people, situation, or parts of myself are involved in the ritual. If the energy I'm dealing with is more amorphous (perhaps I'm feeling uncentered and can't get anything done), I let a scene or symbol float up that represents the root of the problem.

When I find out what it is I want or need to do, I return to breathing deeply in my belly. I turn my attention to the different parts of my body so that I can feel the full power of my energy moving through me. I feel my strength rising inside me as I open up to the energy around me.

I meditate again, asking for symbolic or literal advice. When I see clearly what it is I need to do, I focus on allowing my awareness to flow freely through my body, my surroundings, and everything and everyone connected with the situation. I ring the chimes several times and feel each sound rippling out, carrying the clear energy with it and helping the ritual work.

What I am searching for seems much more possible now, and I sit quietly for a few more minutes, allowing this good feeling to wash over me. I review what I learned in the meditation and determine how I can put it into effect. I thank the spirits within me and without me. To ground my-

self, I tune into my body once again, this time touching myself all over and rubbing my face. I blow out the candles
and, if the incense is still burning, I make sure it is a safe
place.

I get up, stretch, roll, and spend some time digesting the
experience. I go about my life clearer, more focused and
energized, watching and feeling the effects of my ritual unfold. I remember how I felt only an hour ago before the
ritual, and am always amazed at how differently I felt and
how different everything looks now.

Transitions

Rituals are an important way to mark beginnings and
endings, for they can help you focus on completing old aspects of your life so that you are open to new situations.
They can help make a difficult transition more bearable and
emphasize new possibilities, mobilizing energy for a new
project or new phase of your life.

When the person I had lived and traveled with for four
years moved halfway around the world, I had a hard time
going to bed, as I was so used to having someone else there.
I was upset and literally did not know what to do with myself. I started sitting quietly and meditating for a few
minutes at bedtime. It helped me feel centered and gave me
a sense of who I was in my new life. Gradually, this ritual
became an important and valuable part of my life, one that I
could also use in many other situations.

I often do small transitional rituals. Frequently, I stop and
say goodbye to my house when I leave it, sometimes imagining it protected. When I arrive at a gathering, I often spend
a few minutes by myself, breathing or resting my eyes, to get
centered. When I get together with someone, we may hold
hands in silence for a few minutes. This helps us leave behind the busy-ness we may have come from, and focuses us
so that we can be together more fully. If either of us is feeling particularly harassed, we do a little bodywork on one
another.

For a more difficult transition, you may want to find a ritual that you can repeatedly integrate into your daily life.

Relationships: You can do a ritual to mark a transition in a personal relationship. Include as tools in the ritual objects or actions that represent both the old and the new phases of the relationship. If more than one person takes part in the ritual, let each plan part of it. If you have any unfinished business you want to deal with, this is a good time, since you are sharing the common focus of the ritual.

Ask one another, verbally or in a meditation, what you need from one another. If someone has died or gone away, focus on what changes this means in the relationship. How can you work with those changes? Feel the potential for the new relationship.

New beginnings: Rituals are an important way to focus energy when you are starting a new project, job, or phase of your life. Plan the ritual to take place when there is a new moon. You can ask friends to join you in celebrating your move, job, or new phase. Ask them to bring something to share—food to eat, a song, a gift. You can create the ritual with them or they can join you in the ritual you have created.

Houseclearing ritual: Mark off the space by going around and "dusting" out the air with incense, feathers, or gestures. Pour apple cider vinegar into bowls—one for each room. Mix sea salt into each bowl of vinegar (salt is a psychic cleanser). Carry the bowls around the rooms, asking, in your own words, that any unwanted energy from the previous tenants or activity be cleared out and that the space be welcoming and beneficial for the people who will now live, work, and spend time there.

Leave one bowl in each room overnight. The next morning, pour the salt vinegar onto the earth to be reabsorbed.

Trading Rituals

In the olden days, when we needed to do an important ritual we went to the shaman or the priestess or priest for help. Nowadays we can work as one another's shamans, taking turns helping one another make important breakthroughs in our lives. Sometimes this happens spontaneously, or you can plan a ritual exchange.

To trade rituals, find someone who is interested in learning more about them and experiencing new forms. You needn't know anything in particular, just remember the basic form of a ritual: to transform negative energy into positive attitudes. Use your imagination to make up the details.

My friend Leni Schwendinger and I did this for one another and it was one of the most powerful ritual experiences I have ever had. I told Leni I wanted to do a ritual around my house, because I was unhappy about my living situation but could do nothing immediately to change it. Leni encouraged me to talk about my feelings and what I wanted to get out of the ritual. Then she planned the ritual herself, keeping the details a surprise.

I prepared myself that day by clearing out the house and my own feelings as best I could. When Leni arrived, we sat and meditated together. From then on, it was like a series of wonderful games someone had prepared for me. Leni had brought thread to make passageways for me in the house, sequins for lightness that she scattered about, a yellow cellophane heart to shine love in the living room window, and other reminders and meditations to help me feel safe at home. After several hours, the change was miraculous. My eyesight had literally changed, I could see many more colors and I was no longer disturbed. The good effects of the ritual lasted for many months.

Thanksgiving Ritual Meditation Walk

Many rituals are done to ask for something or to get in touch with the universal energy. This meditation ritual is to give thanks for what we have and to thank the energy around us. It was created by Carolyn Shaffer.

Gather together particular tokens from important parts of your life that you can present as gifts. Put on any special clothes that you feel like wearing. Center yourself before you begin. Meditate on all the spirits/energies/friends within and without you who help you. Thank them for all they have done. Thank yourself, too!

Walk around your home, indoors and outdoors. Go to special places and talk to each place, thanking each for what it has given you. Leave one of the tokens in each place as a present. When you are finished, stand in the center and open your arms, feeling the energy moving around you and through you. Feel how you have helped create all that is here for you, and ask that you may continue with new and even more open inspiration.

Don't Get Hooked on Ritual

I love rituals, and I often ritualize something I want to integrate into my daily life. This makes it feel special to me, like a treat, and it gets me doing it—a disguised discipline.

However, at some point, weeks or years later, I start feeling cramped. I have a hard time distinguishing whether I am resisting a breakthrough in a certain practice or whether I have grown beyond the practice, since I started doing it because I wanted to and because it was good for me. It has become part of my life, and I have a hard time letting go of it. Invariably, however, I find that when I feel cramped by a ritual the time has come for me to let the ritual die and move on to something else.

After several experiences of resisting my own impulses and persisting with worn-out rituals, I resolved to try to trust my own instincts more. I realized that ritual is a tool that helps one get in touch with inner and outer forces so that eventually one doesn't need the ritual itself anymore. The more sensitive, aware, and focused we become through ritual, the more we can let go of it and live spontaneously. The purpose of ritual, like any other psychic/psychological/ spiritual tool, is that it should eventually become useless.

Now when one of my rituals dies, I think perhaps a new ritual will be born in its place, or perhaps I will enter into a phase of no rituals, one in which all of my life flows without my conscious effort.

Collective Rituals

Ritual is a powerful community-creating resource. The feeling of shared protection that a ritual creates allows people to open up and be with one another in a unifying way rarely experienced in our culture. The psychic bonding of ritual participants with one another and with nature is one of the most striking aspects of ritual. Like healing, ritual gives us a chance to be open and trusting with one another and allows our true selves to emerge.

We can also use ritual to raise and regenerate our power and direct it towards social and political action. Psychic energy is already mobilized in such work in the collective focus, but often it is not recognized or directed. Frequently it dissipates or becomes internally destructive. The psychic bonding of ritual emphasizes unity and helps people find ways to work together despite their differences. Some of the rituals I like best include personal and group meditations and symbolic actions that focus on a more collective event, such as feminist, environmental, and peace gatherings.

Each participant helps create a collective ritual, whether or not she has helped organize it in advance. A ritual is usually created for each new occasion and no ritual is ever performed the same way twice. Within the created structure, there is always room for flexibility, and participants are usually reminded that they can say or do anything whenever they want. There are no rigid rules or behavior, high priestesses, or superior forces.

Ongoing Ritual Groups

If you can find or create a group to practice ritual regularly, it will help each member of the group develop spiritual skills and give enormous support to the members. You can also integrate ritual in the workings of an existing group. Because ritual is so flexible and emphasizes collectivity, it is a good way to introduce a group of people to new ways of using spiritual power.

A focused, centering way of starting meetings is essential to allow members to relax and to open up psychically to the collective energy of the group. The most common and effective opening ritual is to sit in a circle and hold hands and allow each member to feel connected to the others in the circle (see Chapter 2). This Circle of Hands ritual can be more powerful if each person does a visualization meditation in which she sees a cord linking each person to the others, focusing on a color or sensation traveling around the circle.

You may not be used to holding hands with one another. If this feels uncomfortable to you or your group, try doing it once or twice as an experiment. Touching one another is a way to communicate that is equivalent to communicating verbally. The usual emphasis on verbal contact alone is one cause of breakdown in communication in many groups.

You can also sing! If it's the first meeting, sing one another's names. As your name is being sung, breathe deeply, and notice how much attention you can take. This is also a good way to learn one another's names.

Group Focus on Individual Transitions

Having the group focus on a personal ritual is one important use of collective energies. The group concentration intensifies the individual focus, and a particular person can act as a vehicle for all.

In one ritual workshop, we each brought some problem we wanted to work through ritualistically and took turns working with one another.

Vicki, a psychiatric nurse, wanted to work on her bedtime ritual. She hated getting up to go to work in the morning and discovered that if she focused herself the night before, she awoke looking forward to her day. I suggested she act

out her nighttime ritual, using us as props so that we could
help her develop it. She acted out setting up her altar using
two women as the candles, another woman as the symbolic
object that she put out in the evening to help her focus on
the next day, and another as her inner guide. As she spoke
the affirmations she made to herself about the following
day, we each answered her. She acted out going to sleep and
waking up the next morning. This felt only half complete. I
suggested she do a waking ritual as well to continue the
focus, reviewing the steps of the previous night. This helped
make waking a continuation of the night before and an interesting and engaging experience, rather than the chore it
had been.

Planning a Collective Ritual

You can do a collective ritual with your group. The basic
idea is the same as for individual rituals. You just have more

characters and possibilities. Decide who will organize and lead the ritual—one person or several? If more than one person, decide how you will share responsibility. How will you stay in communication with each other during the ritual? If one person leads, will others help you? You might decide to have each participant come with something to present, or be prepared to create the ritual spontaneously with the group.

Decide on the structure and flow of your ritual. Take into account the attention span of the participants, the time of day, and the weather (especially if your ritual is to be held outside.) How much leeway do you want to allow for improvisation or other spontaneous changes? Agree to trust your intuitions. What ritual tools do you want to use? Using material objects can change an ordinary environment into a ritual space, provide a focus, and establish a relationship between the psychic nature of the ritual and material reality.

You can use candles, incense, symbolic objects, a staff or wand to pass around the group, a goblet for liquids that the participants can drink or use to anoint themselves, a bowl of salt water for ritual cleansing, strips of cloth as banners to dance with, yarn for a bonding cord, food, drink, costumes, masks, face paint. I always like to include something organic —flowers, seashells, water, a branch, fruit, seeds.

The first few times you lead a ritual, you may be convinced that everyone is bored and/or embarrassed for you. (This also happens a lot when you lead a guided meditation, because guided meditation is an unfamiliar experience to most people in our culture and you, as leader, get no immediate response.) Persevere! After the ritual you will probably find out that most of the participants were having a wonderful time. If they weren't, find out why. Responses, both positive and negative, are material for creating future rituals. Recognize that, for their own reasons, some people will not be open to the ritual.

As we create these rituals together, we are learning how to

allow the collective energy to move through us. We are creating new forms, new art, new culture. Most importantly, we are changing the meaning of ritual and bringing it back to life. We are making it possible to call on ourselves and one another to create a ritual for the moment /place/occasion whenever we need to. Our rituals are constantly alive and growing. We all have the power to change any situation we want, but first, we have to discover/remember that power and practice using it.

The Flow of the Ritual

Here are four basic elements to the energy flow of a collective ritual: centering the energy, raising it, directing it, and grounding it. If you don't center and raise the individual and collective energies of the group, you will have nothing to work with. Directing the energy accomplishes your purpose. Grounding the energy means that you don't go away into the everyday world before you are back in an everyday frame of mind.

Centering the Energy

Do a centering exercise or meditation, such as a Circle of Hands, or chanting sounds or one another's names. Then explain the purpose and structure of the ritual. Ask if there are any questions. This allows people to let go of their hesitations and immediately become participants. If the group is unfamiliar with ritual, remind people that they should only participate to the extent that feels comfortable to them. Your explanation helps demystify the ritual for those new to it, gives individuals power, and focuses everyone (including yourself) on your purpose. On a psychic plane, you announce to the forces of the universe that you are about to begin.

• The opening birth arch is a good centering for a group. It is based on the old childhood game of London Bridge. Two women face one another, holding hands with their arms raised above their heads. Another woman steps between them and they drop their arms around her, saying, "By a woman you were born into this world; by women you are born into this circle." They kiss her. Then they raise their arms, she steps forward, and another woman comes under the arch. When she is finished being welcomed, she joins the other woman to form another arch. The other women follow, being welcomed under each arch and forming more arches, until all, including the women of the first arch, have gone through. Then everyone drops hands and each woman takes the hands of the woman on either side of her, forming a circle of hands.

• You can also form a birth canal by standing in a line, one behind the other, with your legs apart. Each person takes a turn lying down on her back and being pulled through the canal by others, who chant and sing her name. Allow yourself to really relax and let the others pull you through the birth canal. When you come out, lie on the floor for a few moments and rest. When you are ready, stand up and join the line so that you can help give birth to the next woman.

Raising the Energy

Do one or more of these: bodywork, chanting, singing, dancing, making music. Bells are good for centering, and drums for raising the energy. Then focus on letting the energy flow around the circle, as in a Circle of Hands.

Directing the Energy

Use movement (including dance), music, words, meditation, or bodywork to transform and direct the energy towards your goal. This process may flow directly from raising the energy.

Cone of power: Stand up and form a circle holding hands. Start the circle revolving by walking, slowly at first, imagining a cone of energy building in the center of the circle. Then move faster and faster, chanting as you go, until everyone senses that the cone overflows and all fall to the floor, visualizing and feeling the energy spilling over them like a fountain, as each person takes what she needs.

Feeding one another: Pass around seed, fruit, or water that has been "charged" with the power of the women present. (You can charge water, food, or inanimate objects by focusing or directing your energy towards it, through a meditation or laying on of hands.) Each women feeds another, so that all feel the food nourishing their bodies to create whatever personal or collective energy they want. As each woman takes her turn, she can announce to the group, in the present tense, an affirmative statement of what energy she is planting within herself: "With this seed I plant in myself a reneweal of my energy to (nourish myself and others, eradicate violence, and so on). As I watch the seeds in the ground grow, blossom, and bear fruit, so I will feel this energy rising in me." This is a wonderful reclaiming of the Christian communion ritual. We are all the "priestesses" and we feed one another from the body of the earth—undoubtedly the original communion.

Creating an altar: Each person takes a turn stepping into the center of the circle. She expresses her contribution to the ritual, as well as her purpose in being there, by placing an object in the center and explaining its significance in words, movement, or song.

Lifting one another: As described in Chapter 5, this is good for a general group ritual as a way of honoring one another, developing trust, providing a safe, loving space, and practicing healing. A woman lies down and everyone else places their hands underneath her (five people or more can easily lift one person). Slowly, they lift her to shoulder height or above their heads, rock her back and forth, and chant her name. They lower her to the ground and, after resting a bit, take their turns.

Psychic cleansing: Salt water is the traditional psychic cleanser. If there is any negative energy the group wants to get rid of (such as disharmony among the participants that is too extreme to be dealt with only verbally), pass around a bowl of salt water. Each person imagines that she is pouring her unwanted energy into the water and announces it to the group. "I put in anger . . . distrust . . . doubt . . . competitiveness." At some point, each woman drinks from the water, feeling the energy—transmuted by the salt cleansing into a positive force— entering her and the group. "I feel my energy transmuted to strength . . . cooperation . . . joy . . . confidence."

Giving someone energy: If one person is the focus of the ritual, send energy to her through a circle of hands. Feel the energy coursing around the circle, each person giving what she can, and taking what she needs.

Sharing: Allot some time in the ritual for anyone who wants to share her visions, ideas, feelings. You can pass around a symbolic object to signify who has the attention of the group. This could be a gourd "rattle," as in Native American rituals, a branch, staff, shell, or anything else that has significance for the group. Sometimes many people may participate in this way, sometimes none. If too much time is being taken up with sharing, you can ask how the group is feeling and suggest that you continue with the rest of the planned ritual and share afterwards.

You may want to make the bulk of the ritual free time, in which everyone brings something to share. This can be the best kind of ritual, for everyone is equally participant and leader. Seeing all the contributions fitting together is an exciting and beautiful ritual experience. It always astounds me how somehow—magically, psychically—we individually emphasize similar themes and how someone will speak up offering a song, dance, or idea just when one is needed.

Closing the Circle

It is important to ground the energy before everyone leaves a ritual. This is known as "closing the circle." Ritual energy is a very powerful force, psychically, psychologically, and materially. A definite closing is needed to make sure that the individuals and the group do not leave feeling spaced out, speedy, or still in a special state in a world that doesn't validate it.

You can ground the energy by any of the means you used

to raise it—meditation, movement, chanting. Using an element similar to that used in the beginning of the ritual can enhance the sense of completion. At the end, focus on quieting, centering, and internalizing the energy you raised, as well as deciding on and visualizing the concrete ways you will use that energy in the future.

The connection we make between the ritual space and the everyday world is an essential element of ritual. I always incorporate some form of this guided meditation:

"Notice how you feel different from the way you did before the ritual. Feel, visualize, and project how you will feel, act, and be as a result of the ritual . . . when you walk away . . . a week from now . . . a year from now. Feel your strength. What is one concrete way that you will continue the energy of the ritual?"

I then do some concrete action to further ground the energy, such as one of the following:

• The closing birth arch is the reverse of the opening birth arch mentioned earlier. This time say: "By women you were born into this circle. By women you are born into the world."

• Then lean over and place your palms on the ground. Imagine that you are opening your hands and feet to the earth and let any excess energy flow out of them into her. She can absorb and transmute it. Thank the environment.

• If you have created a collective altar, each woman retrieves her contribution and thanks the group for investing its energy in her object.

• Pick yarn, cord, or string of an appropriate color. (Red for menstruation and power, green for spring and rebirth—whatever color you intuit is best. I am always drawn to reddish-purple.) At some point in the ritual, pass it around the circle. As each woman winds it around the waist of the woman next to her, she proclaims (aloud or silently) what energy she is generating. Continue until all in the circle are bound with the cord. Tie the loose ends together to represent the umbilical cord that unites us all. The cord will continue to absorb the

energy as the ritual goes on. You can do a guided meditation, chant, sing, or take turns speaking while the cord surrounds you. When you are ready to end the ritual, each person cuts or tears the cord. If you use yarn, you can untwist it and pull it apart, as some Native American weavers do. Each person ties the piece of cord around some part—throat, wrist, waist— of the woman next to her, or gives it to her to carry.

After the ritual, everyone will carry with her a highly charged reminder of the psychic energy of the ritual. You will be connected by the same umbilical cord. It's fun to recognize other people wearing their cords. Wear the cord as long as it feels right, and when you take it off, keep it in a special place, use it to make something, or burn it.

• I always close a ritual with an energy circle. Ground and center yourselves as in the beginning of the ritual. Chant or sing—let your throats be open with all the energy you have raised. Say a blessing such as: "The circle is open, but unbroken. Merry meet and merry part, and merry meet again. Blessed Be."

Experiencing the psychic energies of a group can be like a day-long hike— exhilarating, cleansing, and exhausting. Be sure to allow time to rest so that you can integrate all the powers you have raised.

A Work Ritual

Here is a description by one woman of a ritual I helped her plan for a group of women she worked with:

Since I'd never done anything like this at all, I was embarrassed and holding back some. Also, I was worried about how people were going to take it, so I didn't want to look like I was taking it too seriously. Sharon joked and called me a swami—laughing made us all feel easier about it.

One thing I had people do was the candle ritual. I carved ten stars— one for each member of the company— on the candle we lit at the beginning of the weekend. I said that as the candle melted down and all the wax of the stars ran together, it symbolized all of us uniting. For the candle we lit at the end, I had a better idea: I had each person carve her own star on it!

We also did the bowl of salt water ritual. It was incredible to hear all the things people poured into it: anger, fear, laziness, self-doubt, competitiveness. . . . All those things we're not supposed to feel that of course everyone does, although they hide them most of the time. People couldn't stop passing around the bowl of water—it just kept going round and round the circle and each person really got a chance to express herself. It was wonderful hearing the responses from the others as we each revealed her "negative" parts. As each "negativity" was dumped into the bowl, the others would cheer and say, "Oh yes!" and "Me too!"

Doing the cord ritual meant a lot. People wore their cords for a long time. Next time we'll use a nicer material so they'll last longer. I've still got mine—it feels really good to have it close to me. I attached a special pendant on it.

I'd like to keep on doing rituals and make this kind of retreat a yearly thing, because it really helps us work together.

You might say that the kind of group we are is the kind who would be most resistant to any kind of spiritual work. I know that's how I felt for a long time. But, we're really looking for and needing unity in order to survive. After a while of working together, we found that in order to really stay united on a deep level, we had to do some things many of us had previously discounted, use some tools like ritual that we've found really *do* work. The rituals we did really symbolized and concretized the unity that was the focus of the retreat.

I think a lot of us have spirituality in us but don't know how to express it or are embarrassed by it because we have rejected the old forms. But we still need something to fill in the gaps. People really do like being spiritual. I know that I enjoy it and I'd like to develop it more now. I learned a lot leading those rituals. Next time, I'll feel more comfortable. It'll probably be easier for all of us.

7. Living in Harmony

> Serving fire,
> At Winter Solstice, kindling new life
> With sparks of the old
> From black coals of the old,
> Seeing them glow again,
> Shuddering with the mystery,
> We know the terror of rebirth.
>
> From *"Chains of Fire,"*
> by ELSA GIDLOW*

As we come to the close of this millenium, an essential part of our development is recognizing our place as co-creators with other forms of life. To survive, we must learn to acknowledge, understand and work with the rest of the planet and universe. We are a part of the earth, and our greatest potential for creating lies in recognizing and working with natural forces. These forces manifest themselves in many ways: through the energy in our hands, the cycles of nature and human life, the healing power of herbs, food and the elements, the psychic energy of meditation, and the application of our art and vision in everyday life.

Women, whose bodies reflect the cycles of the moon and who are able to create new life, seem to have a more instinc-

---

*See p. xv for entire poem. Elsa Gidlow, age eighty-four, whose birthday is at the Winter Solstice, gathers friends every year and lights her Winter Solstice fire with a log from the previous Solstice's fire. She writes in her autobiography-in-progress, "I started when I acquired my first own hearth in 1941. I kept the residue of that first fire and have lighted the Solstice fires thereafter each year from the previous year's charcoal. I like the feeling of continuity, not only with the years of my own life but with all past women. The poem was not written until 1954, when it seemed to emerge one dawn almost of itself as I lighted my regular morning fire."

tive understanding of the interdependence of all creation. Thus we find ourselves in a unique position to lead the way in the search for more holistic and health-giving forms of thinking, living, and acting. We have the power to help transform the hierarchy that sets mind above body, man above woman, human above nature.

Our Whole Selves

One way we can begin to heal this imbalance is to heal ourselves. It is important that we work on all levels—with our bodies, our dreams, our history, our mythology, our meditations, and our rituals—and that we integrate this work with our own cycles and those of nature. All of these approaches affect different parts of ourselves. If we neglect any of them, we neglect that part of ourselves and the rest suffers as well.

Healing Your Whole Self

• Set aside some time for yourself to meditate.
• Use basic relaxation, inner guidework, or any other technique that works for you to get into a meditative state.
• Ask yourself questions about factors that affect your health. What is your living situation? Is it what you want, or are there changes you would like to make? Are you willing to make them? What emotions have you been experiencing? What's on your mind? What's your health been like? Have you been getting enough sleep? Eating well? Exercising? What has your psychic life been like lately—your dreams, meditations, intuitions? How does your spiritual life affect your everyday life? Your relationships? Your ability to effect change in the world? How are these different things related? Do you notice any patterns of connection between the different parts of your life? How can you integrate your spiritual life more with the rest of your life?
Think about another time in your life. Take the first one

that pops into your mind and see if you notice any similarities between then and now.

• Imagine that you go inside yourself and have a dialogue with the part of yourself that doesn't feel well. What does it say to you? What is blocking your health? What does the ailing part of you need? Do you want to make those changes? Accept and affirm the answers you find within yourself.

• Imagine that each time you inhale, you are sending warmth and love to the part of you that is being healed or worked on. Feel this energy streaming throughout your body. Feel the connection of all your parts. Realize that you are a whole, healthy, and creative being. *Know* that you are an integral part of the life-flow of the universe. Allow its energy to flow through you, cleansing you, healing you, revitalizing you. Imagine this feeling of health radiating throughout the room, building, neighborhood, state, country, and planet. You begin with yourself, move throughout the world, and come full circle once again to your own individual place in the cosmos.

• When you are ready, touch yourself all over your body, feeling the healing energy you send yourself. Slowly sit up and hug yourself.

NOTES

Meditating on the Elements

According to Gandhi, five basic elements of nature move through our bodies and the world around us: earth, air, fire, water, and ether (space). Without them we cannot survive. Throughout most of human existence, and particularly in prepatriarchal times, people have been conscious of their dependency on the elements to a much greater degree than we are. You can re-establish your relationship to the elements. It may sound old-fashioned, but it works!

Earth Meditation

We literally need to ground ourselves every day by making some contact with the earth. We can do this by spending some time in nature—what I call the "real world."

• Find a time and place to be out in the real world. Go outdoors, take a walk or a lunch break in a park. Notice what is around you: trees, plants, sky, birds, grass. Take a few deep breaths. As you gaze at your surroundings, allow the colors and life of what you see to sink into your eyes, into your mind, and down through your body. Let yourself really be with them, not just staring at them or thinking about them or other things. Let yourself be fed by the mother earth. Feel your contact with her through your feet. Imagine a cord connecting you at the navel with the center of the earth. Let her energy flow through you. Know that you are part of her and she part of you. Touch the earth. What do you feel? When you leave, say goodbye to the trees, flowers, birds, sky. Thank them. Tell them you will be back later.

Exercise is a way of connecting with the earth as manifested in you—your physical body. We need some exercise every day to get the blood flowing and to get ourselves out of our heads. Recent scientific discoveries have shown that after ten or twelve minutes of vigorous exercise particular chemicals that are associated with happiness are produced in the body.

There are many ways to get your energy flowing through exercise. The point is not to do it just because it is good for you, but because it feels good, because you enjoy it, because you are learning something from it, because it is a meditation for you, and so on. Let your exercise—walking, gardening, physical labor, running, dance, movement, martial arts, yoga, swimming, whatever—become an integral and enjoyable part of your life. It may become your favorite part of the day.

Air Meditation

To Hindu yogis, breath, or *prana,* is the same as energy. We can survive for hours and even days without food, water, sleep, or light, but we can do without air for only a few minutes.

As we breathe, taking in the oxygen that gives life to our cells, we can feel in a tangible way the energy of the universe in all parts of our bodies. Breath awareness allows us to rediscover the natural rhythm of breathing and to explore our bodies with our breath.

Notice how you breathe in different emotional situations and when you block your breath. When you are upset, think about how to allow your breath-energy to move more freely. Imagine that you send your breath to different parts of your body, to soothe and release it from tension.

• There are many different approaches to breathing. Most important is that you *do* breathe (most of us only breathe partially). This means letting your spine and chest be free, noticing when you hold your breath, and taking a few deep breaths, sighs, or yawns regularly. If you allow your breath to follow its own natural course, you will gradually be able to breathe more fully.

• You can use your breath directly for healing (see Basic Relaxing Meditation, Chapter 2), as did this woman: "When I jumped out of the tree and heard my ankle turn, I prepared myself for great pain, for it was the ankle I had sprained several times before. Then I remembered about breathing into it, sending all the blood and oxygen and relaxing energy I could into it. I imagined breathing into the ankle for about half an hour, and by the end of that time the swelling, which had been the size of a tennis ball, had almost completely gone down! It completely healed in three days, rather than the week it would normally take."

• Being consistent about breathing means getting out into the country, parks, mountains, ocean, or desert where you can breathe fresh air. Run, hike, or exercise while you are there so that your lungs and the rest of your body can clean out and rediscover their capacity. If you smoke, examine why you do, what it does for you, how it affects your breathing, and whether you want to continue.

I smoked cigarettes for eight years, a pack a day for four of them. I was surprised to find out several years after I quit, through a chest x-ray, that my lungs were completely cleaned out. I attributed this in part to the year of yoga breathing exercises I had done since I had stopped smoking.

Fire Meditation

Through the sun and moon, fire and its light are ever-present in our lives. Most people in the world continually interact with natural fire as they use it for heat and cooking. Natural light is essential for growth and health because it stimulates the pineal and pituitary glands. Artificial lighting, living behind windows and car windshields, watching television, and wearing sunglasses, contact lenses, or prescription glasses that do not allow the full spectrum of light into the eye all affect our health.

• To allow your body to maintain as much of its natural balance as possible, spend as much time as you can out of doors with as little clothing as possible, not necessarily in the full sun. Too much sun can be as bad as too little. If you wear glasses or contact lenses, take them off when you don't need them. This allows more of the natural light to come in. After a while, you will find you need them less than you thought.

• "Sun" your eyes several times a day. Close your eyes, turn your face towards the sun, and slowly move it back and forth. Do this about ten times. Turn away from the sun and lie with your eyes closed. Then slowly open them. This practice exposes your eyes to the natural light. It also relaxes your eyes so that they allow more light to enter.

• Try to sleep so that moonlight falls on you. If you can, sleep outside. "Moon" your eyes by closing them, facing the moon, and slowly turning your head from side to side.

• Meditate on a candle. Watch it for several minutes. Imagine the light of the candle growing larger and larger until it fills the whole room, including your body, washing it with light. How do you feel? What does it say to you about light and your needs for light in the rest of your life?

Water Meditation

Much of our bodies are made up of water. Life originally emerged from the sea herself. Immersing any part of ourselves in water changes the electromagnetic currents of our bodies. Many European health spas use various water cures as part of their natural healing, often with dramatic results.

Here's how you can do your own water cure:

• Take a hot bath. Ritualize it with candles, incense, and music.

• Take a shower or go to a waterfall or the ocean. Electric negative ions, which are depleted in cities, are plentiful near moving water. The lack of negative ions can cause both physical and mental sickness.

• Drink water! Preferably, you should drink spring water or purified spring water or purified tap water. Drinking four to eight cups of water a day (instead of relying on coffee, juices, milk, soft drinks, or alcoholic beverages) flushes out your system—and helps prevent cystitis, the bladder infection so common in women.

Space Meditation

For the first fifty thousand or more years of human existence, there were very few people on the planet earth. In only the last few hundred years, that number has grown to such a degree that we are rapidly crowding ourselves out. In addition, we have a corresponding growth of buildings, machines, noise, and concrete. The ever-diminishing amount of space that each of us has affects our physical, emotional, and mental health. We forget about other forms of life. We become human chauvinists.

Find ways that you can develop more space—both inside and outside yourself.

• Spend a day in some open space alone.

• Meditate to open up your inner spaces.

• Consider carefully before contributing to the population explosion of humans and machines. Make space in your life for animals, plants, air, water, earth, and heavenly bodies.

• Meditate on the sky. Let it give you a perspective on yourself and the role of human beings in the universe. Sweep your eyes all along the horizon. Look straight above you. Look at other parts of the sky. What do you see? How is it different from yesterday? How does it make you feel? Do you remember what the sky looked like when you were younger? Do you have memories of special skies? What effect did it have on you? When there is a storm, sit and watch the clouds, snow, rain, hail, or lightning. Close your eyes and feel your inner space. How does it feel compared with the space that is out there?

• Night sky. Go somewhere where the air is relatively clear. Lie down on your back and watch the blackness, the stars, the clouds, the moon. How do they make you feel? Feel their expansiveness moving through your head, chest, belly, through your limbs. Feel the stars within you.

Nourishing Yourself

Women have long been associated with food and nourishment, yet more recently this role has been less valued than before. Food has become a complex problem for many women, as we have been encouraged to feed others and starve ourselves to be "beautiful." We need to learn how to listen to our own bodies in order to nourish ourselves. Doing this meditation can help you distinguish between foods your body wants, foods your soul wants, and foods that you think you "should" want or that advertisers encourage you to want. You may also find that there are times when you need emotional nourishment, not food. You can learn to be sensitive to what foods and amounts of foods are right for you at different times.

• Find some time when you can eat in peace. Plan to eat food that has been prepared by yourself or by friends. You can go to a favorite room, outdoors, or take a picnic with other people. If you are with others, begin by doing a Circle of Hands, with the food in the center of the circle. If you are alone, place the food in front of you, in your lap, or hold it.

• Hold your hands over or around your food. Close your eyes. Center yourself by taking a few deep breaths and then relaxing with your breathing. Sit with your hands over your food and imagine that you exchange energy with it. This helps equalize the balance between you and your food so that it is more easily assimilated by your body.

• Thank each different ingredient. Thank the earth for giving it to you. Feel the earth that is under you. Allow her energy to travel up your spine. Become aware of all the power and life that creates your food: the minerals and nutrients in the soil, the worms and other insects that feed the soil, the trees and other plants that provide shade and compost for your food, the moon and sun and rain that vitalize it. Realize that you are a part of the earth—that her food is continually feeding you and replenishing your bones, muscles, blood, organs, skin, brain. Feel how much of this energy you can absorb directly from the elements.

• Realize that we are all part of a continuous cycle: we are fed by the plants that are all around us, when we die our bodies compost to feed them, other people and animals eat the plants, they die, and on and on. Allow yourself to open to this never-ending cycle of energy. Know that you are continually grow-ing, dying, and being reborn.

• Tune in to the food. What kind of feeling are you getting from it? Is your body ready for it? Do you want to eat it? Are there other ways you can nourish yourself? What do your reactions tell you about your eating habits and your health?

• When you are ready, slowly open your eyes. Look around you. What do you see? Who do you see? When you want, feed yourself or one another, beginning in silence. Let yourself eat in a new way—sucking, tasting, being fed, licking. Eat with your hands.

• Feel the energy of the earth, plants, moon, and sun travel-ing through you as you eat your food. Eat what you need, what you want, when you want.

• Chew every bite fifty times so that the food becomes liquid and the digestive juices of your saliva can get a chance to help you digest it. Sip liquids. There's an old saying: "Drink what you eat and eat what you drink."

• Whenever you eat, make a ritual of nourishing your body. Choose a favorite bowl or plate as your ritual implement. When you are finished eating, carefully wash and dry your tools and put them away.

Your Cycles

The cyclic energy of the universe is reflected in the ebb and flow of the tides, the moon's waxing and waning, the changing seasons, and the patterns of day and night. Our own cycles of birth, growth and change, and death are part of the larger natural cycles. Understanding and working with our cycles is an essential part of working with energy, natural healing, and preventive medicine.

Modern industrial society almost completely ignores natu-ral cycles and tries to force life into an artificial linear struc-ture. We are not able to use our energy to the fullest because we do not recognize the subtlety and variety of the cyclic energy flowing through us. We often become sick from ignoring our own cycles, or we *think* we are sick because our energy fluctuates.

Knowing about your cycles and working with them will help you get more done, conserve your energy, and make your life generally more peaceful. Respecting cycles is like swimming with the tide rather than against it.

Frequent human cycles are most evident in women's lunar menstrual cycles. In addition to the physical changes, we are usually more or less psychic, sensitive, and sexual in response to menstruation and ovulation. In nontechnological cultures, such as the Native American, a woman often stops working during her period, retires to a moon-hut, and focuses all her attention on her increased psychic abilities. In patriarchal times, this "retreat" began to be imposed upon women as a *taboo* (literally, "sacred") due to fear of the creative power symbolized by women's periodic blood.

Women in modern technological societies tend to be irritable during their periods and to have painful cramps for several reasons. Bad diet can make cramps worse. Hatred and fear of women and menstruation causes psychological and physiological stress. In addition, at a time when our bodies want to rest and our psychic selves are demanding more attention, we are forced to continue our normal, outer-directed, more stressful lives.

Our obvious cycles are seen as a weakness; we resist them, generate stress, and turn a natural cycle into a sickness. Ignoring menstrual cycles is one of the most obvious instances of creating disease by regimenting our lives—but both men and women suffer many abuses of the cyclical nature of human life. We can begin to alleviate discomfort and to transform it into positive energy for ourselves by becoming familiar with and respectful of our bodies and their cycles and by living more in harmony with them.

Start noticing your different cycles—menstruation, sleeping, physical energy, moods, sexuality, mental focus, psychic experiences, dreams. Make a chart with a column for each cycle and mark days or weeks, using different colors, numbers, or symbols to record your changes. You can use a lunar calendar (available at feminist, spiritual, or other bookstores) to compare your cycles to those of the moon. By learning your own cycles, you can prepare for them, use your energy to its fullest, and better understand and accept yourself. Try not to judge your fluctations; feeling low physically may give you the opportunity to be quiet, reflective, creative, or make an important decision.

If you are menstruating, spend the first day as quietly as possible, with few outside demands or distractions. If you must go to work, stay aware of your body and its needs. Move, stretch, breathe deeply, and take time for yourself as much as possible. Give yourself time to work with your dreams, meditate, and be creative. Make this a time to pay attention to your innermost self and your own special relationship with nature.

Rituals for Natural Cycles

Some of the most important elements of reclaiming our roles as creation makers are recognizing, affirming, and respecting the natural cycles of birth, growth, death, and rebirth. These cycles are reflected in the stages of human life, the rising and setting of the sun and moon, the phases of the moon, and the changing seasons. Nature provides us endless opportunities to remember her cycles, to celebrate them, and to experience our own changes with hers.

Practicing regular cyclic rituals helps us stay in touch with the energy flow of the natural world in which we live—a connection we need in a technological society. Doing rituals for the different stages of our lives helps us make the inevitable transitions more smoothly and wisely. Such rituals are also good preventive medicine; by recognizing our own cycles of change, we promote our physical, emotional, and spiritual well-being.

Seasonal Rituals

As we celebrate the cycles of the earth, we celebrate our own cycles. In the spring and summer, our energy is outer-directed. In the fall and winter, we turn inward and harvest the fruit of the seeds we planted earlier. The Winter Solstice takes us on an internal journey to synthesize, comprehend, and focus the outer-directed experiences of the previous spring and summer. We use this new understanding as a guide for our actions and vision in the following spring and summer, the next turn of the spiral. We are continually gathering, synthesizing, building, turning in the cycles of the year and of our own growth.*

To create any seasonal ritual, think of what is important to you about the time of the year or month. What is going on in the material world? The earth? Moon? Sun? What changes are going on in you or in your group? What is the correspondence between the people and nature?

Design a ritual that celebrates the changes inside and outside you. Include meditation, movement, natural objects that encompass the occasion of your ritual. I celebrate the traditional European seasonal rituals, based on the cycles of the earth. They are:

Spring Equinox: Around March 20—days and nights are of equal length—time of celebrating rebirth and the reunion of Persephone and Demeter. Symbols: eggs, (they balance on end at this time of year) new growth, colors green and yellow.

May 1: Also known as Beltane—beginning of good weather. Symbols: Maypole, flowers.

Summer Solstice: Around June 20—the longest day of the year and the height of outer-directed activity—celebrate Midsummer's Eve now with the nature spirits.

---

*See Eleanor C. Merry, *The Year and Its Festivals* (London: Anthroposophical Publishing Company, 1952).

Lammas: August 1—beginning of the harvest, both material and spiritual—beginning to prepare for the inner-directedness of the winter.

Fall Equinox: Around September 21—day and night of equal length—height of the harvest and laying up of stores.

Hallomas: October 31—time of increasing darkness and moon- and starlight—dedicated to the goddess of night and death, Hecate—extremely potent time for psychic work and transcending the barriers between the seen and unseen worlds.

Winter Solstice: Around December 21—longest night of the year—a time for celebrating the quiet reflective times of darkness—celebrating the rebirth of the Sun Goddess.

Candlemas: February 2—days rapidly become longer—time of initiations.

Here's a sample invocation for the Winter Solstice:

"The Sun Goddess, Juno Lucina of Rome, Atthar of Arabia, Amaterasu of Japan, is reborn! From the Winter

Solstice on, she rises higher and higher in the sky. With her festival, we celebrate the cycles of the earth, the hibernation of the animals, the intense energy of the seeds as they prepare to burst forth above the earth. This Winter Solstice, we look back to the Summer Solstice, feel our strength, and see how we have grown and how we will continue to grow. We feel our strength, our beauty, our power! The goddess in each of us is reborn to a new cycle."*

Birth Ritual

Birth rituals are probably the oldest women's rituals. We need to create new ones to replace modern practices so that women can give birth as consciously as possible.

This ritual, created by Carolyn Shaffer and myself for our friend Ruth Eckland, is to be done soon before a woman is to give birth to a physical child or to a creative project. Close friends of the woman plan to gather with her. Each attunes herself beforehand by meditating on the nature of birth, the changes in her own life, and her relationship to the mother and the child to be born. This is an opportunity for the mother to stop and acknowledge, both to herself and with the focussed attention of her friends, the fact that she is about to go through a major transition.

• You will need to bring: a ball of reddish yarn or string, cornmeal, cloth and bowl for washing, the mother's hairbrush, and red eggs. Prepare the eggs by hard-boiling and then peeling them. Soak the peeled eggs overnight with cooked beets or beet juice, so that the dye from the beets colors the eggs. Guests may also bring food to share and presents for the mother or child. During the ritual, the mother will wear a robe that she will also wear while she is giving birth.

---

*For more suggestions on European-American pagan rituals, see Starhawk, *The Spiral Dance: A Rebirth of the Ancient Religion of the Great Goddess* (San Francisco: Harper & Row, 1979) and Z. Budapest, *The Holy Book of Women's Mysteries* (Oakland, California: Susan B. Anthony Coven #1, 1979).

• When all are gathered, take some time to do a centering meditation holding hands. Let one woman explain the process of the ritual to the group. Take the ball of yarn and pass it throughout the circle, affirming the power of the psychic umbilical cord uniting all present, and the woman's ability to give birth.

• When this is done, let one woman rub the mother's feet in cornmeal while another brushes her hair. This a Native American custom, and women say that it makes them feel nourished and cared for at the time when they are giving, and preparing to give, so much nourishment. At this time, her friends may speak affirmations to her of her strength and her ability to receive love. The mother may talk openly about her feelings about the birth and receive support from the group for them. Finally, her feet are washed clean.

Pass around the eggs in a bowl so each can take one. Let each woman hold her egg in her hands and meditate on what gift she would like the egg to represent. Starting with the mother, the bowl is passed around and each woman cuts up her egg into it, saying what powers she would like to invoke for the mother, the unborn child, and for all present. Eggs that have been dyed in beet juice are beautiful, so allow time for each woman to appreciate the vision.

• When all are finished, you may sit and hold hands and chant or sing, meditating on the birth of new energy each is experiencing in her life.

• When ready, pass around the bowl of eggs, each woman feeding the one next to her.

• Close the ritual by breaking the yarn wrapped around you and tying it around your wrist or waist. You may then celebrate with gift-giving, food-sharing, talking, singing, and dancing or massage.

Moon Rituals

Many women attune their rituals to the cycles of the moon. The new moon is a time for new beginnings, and you can see the first crescent moon in the western sky just after sunset. At the full moon, which rises just as the sun is setting, you can do rituals for celebrating and completing a cycle.

For thousands of years, women's menstrual blood has been revered as a symbol of her overt connection with heavenly bodies, her ability to bleed without dying, and her life-creating power. This power is so immense that, in the patriarchy, that respect has turned into fear. The original meaning of *taboo* —"sacred"—has been changed to "forbidden." An essential step in reclaiming our spiritual power, as well as knowledge of and control of our bodies, is learning not to hate and fear our menstrual blood. For a young girl's first menstruation, welcome it as do women in traditional cultures: with rituals, congratulations and celebration.

You can do both a private retreat and a more public acknowledgment of a girl's maturing to womanhood. Mother and daughter, along with other women (some girls find it easier to learn from or talk with women from outside their families) may go away together to a private place, preferably in the country. Try to plan the retreat for the three days at the dark or full moon. Spend as much time as possible out of doors, perhaps staying up all one night under the full moon. The structure of the retreat may be quite informal, with an emphasis on the time spent together, on communicating with one another, and on acknowledging the cycles of human life and of nature. The older women may tell stories of their own lives, their transition to womanhood, the joys and difficulties, important women in their lives, and so on. The younger women may do the same, including talking about what they are experiencing at the present and their hopes and fears for the future. You may end the retreat with a ritual and feast. In Bali the girl is offered food representing the range of life's experiences: sweet, bitter, and so forth.

When you return to your homes, you may want to acknowledge to your community this passage into womanhood with a ritual, a party, the taking on of responsibilities and privileges, or whatever else you mutually decide upon. Women who have done such retreats and ceremonies find that they open up doors to increased communication and that the effects of the retreat, in particular, unfold over the years.*

Aging Ritual

Mary Lee George created this ritual to acknowledge and affirm her aging from mature woman to crone, a traditional title for an old woman:

I lit three candles—one white for youth, one red for middle age, and one black for the Crone. I danced for the intimate group of women whom I had invited to witness my crone crossing. When the dance was finished, I blew out all the candles so that we were in darkness. We meditated on being in darkness.

Each woman had been given a candle, so to bring us out of darkness, I lit my candle and passed its light on to the woman next to me, saying, "I am a woman and I give you creative energy." The woman with the second lighted candle then passed it on to the woman next to her repeating, "I am a woman and I give you serenity (or whatever came in mind that that woman needed/wanted). The light and phrase, "I am a woman and I give you ... " were passed on to all the rest of the women in the circle until it came back to me and each woman held a lighted candle.

We honored many of the crones who had been important in our lives, both those who were no longer alive and those who were. I asked for the energy of the dead crones to bless us and be with us. I sent energy to the crones who are still alive and asked for their energy to be with us. Each one who wished to honor a crone said her name out loud and something about her. Many of us mentioned our mothers, grandmothers, and aunts. This was followed by a time for sharing our fears and hopes about getting older. I talked about both the pain and the advantages that come when one is older. My friends gave me symbols that they had brought to ease

---

*Thanks to Yvonne Rand for her suggestions.

my transition: among them were some black candles, a snake bracelet made from a root, a plant, some wine, and a wonderful color photograph of a mushroom which I call Venus of Willendorf. We ended by drinking herbal tea and singing.

Death Ritual

Death is one of the major transitions of our lives. In many societies, such as the present-day Tibetan and the ancient Egyptian and Catal Huyuk cultures, death seems to have been an important event to be prepared for consciously and without fear. Yet in most modern death rituals, which employ only undertakers and funeral services, the powerful emotional and psychic aspects of death are dealt with inadequately.

Our culture promotes fear of death—the huge medical industries that prolong "life" at all economic, emotional, physical, and psychic costs; the cosmetic and beauty industries that promote youth; and the funeral industry, which takes over at the moment of death. On a spiritual level our fear of change, of psychic death and rebirth, keeps us from personal development and growth and from political action.

Death is hardly talked about until it occurs, and then it is treated with ignorance and fear. Morticians take care of the physical aspects of it, priests the spiritual, while the survivors sit by helplessly, with little opportunity to express or direct their feelings. Most particularly, death is seen only as an ending and as a loss, rather than as the transformation and renewal of energy that it is.

We have forgotten death's association with birth and rebirth. In death, we return to the womb of the earth mother, to enter once again the collective energy of the universe. Our alienation from this force has made us ignorant of and fearful of death, as well as of the cosmos itself. It is hard to talk about death, since we are so ignorant about it. Part of our work is to begin to understand and live with death, so that we can live with and understand life better.

Reclaiming our own death rituals is an essential beginning. I see women ritualizing death in a way that is exceed-
ingly beautiful and startling in its creativity and power. The
focus is on understanding death, helping the dying person
remain as conscious and fearless as possible, and directing
energy towards the dead person. We are learning to express
and honor the range of our emotions—hurt, shock, anger,
guilt, sorrow, loss, resentment.

Doing a Death Ritual

Try to plan your ritual for the third day after the death.
In many mythologies, this is the time of the completion of
the separation of the spirit/soul/energy from the body. This
time span also coincides with the three-day "death" of the
dark of the moon. If you can't have the ritual three days
after the death, that's fine. The intent is more important
than the timing. If some people can't come to the ritual, ask
them to sit quietly wherever they are and join your circle in
meditation while you are having it.

Ask everyone who comes to bring something to share. It
can be material or nonmaterial—a poem, song, memory,
meditation, object, and so on. In one ritual, we found that
we had all brought a talisman for the wife of the dead man
to help her take the body back to the man's family and go
through the funeral. You may want to wear special clothes
or bring special foods. Prepare the space by cleaning it,
meditating, walking around with incense, and so on. Empty
yourself of any preconceptions of what will or should happen.

When everyone has arrived, sit in a circle and hold hands.
Each person "checks in," saying briefly how she is feeling.
Let one person lead the others in a meditation to transform
any negative feelings into positive ones (grief is not necessarily negative). Direct your attention towards the person
who has died. Focus on where she is now—whether in a personal form, as a soul, or as more amorphous energy. What is

the essence of her energy? Imagine her ridding herself of the past. Let her be reborn. You can say out loud what you are feeling, so that a collective vision emerges.

Direct your efforts toward helping the person through this transition. When this feels complete, let awareness flow around the circle once again, this time focusing on receiving energy to help yourselves through the transition. Feel what is dying and being reborn in you.

Let each person say what part of her or her relationship with the dead person is now complete and what is being reborn. Allow yourselves to feel the energy pouring new life into you. When you are ready, end the meditation and open your eyes. Hug one another, rub one another's shoulders, and share your feelings.

Next, take turns sharing whatever you brought for the ritual. Gradually, the ritual will become more of an unstructured coming together. Enjoy it, celebrate your new rebirth, and particularly your feeling of community. Think of the tradition of the Irish wakes. Before you leave, hold hands in the circle to center yourselves and to ground the energy. "Merry meet, merry part, and merry meet again!"

This excerpt from my journal describes my first reactions to a death ritual:

Glenna has been murdered. She was shot through the chest by a robber. I can hardly believe that as I write it. *Why?* I feel as though my whole universe has been shattered. Anger, rage, shock, disbelief, love, helplessness, sorrow, horror are all so real. I am living in a world of raging emotions and no idea what to do with them.

Glenna—twenty-three years old. My friends and I were so excited to have found her as a friend and for her work as an excellent psychic. She has helped a lot of us and we were beginning to bring new experiences into her life. Some of us organized a ritual for her and to support Briana, her sister, who was her assistant and is taking the body back to their parents'.

We come together at my house. Some of us don't know one another. We do a circle of hands and each say briefly how she is feeling. Then we do a meditation together to focus on sending energy to Glenna.

I visualize Glenna. Amazingly, I see her happy. She tells me that she is okay, that she feels held back by sorrow, doesn't want to be—she wants to move on.... We talk awhile. "Glenna, I love you," I say, and feel myself releasing my hold on her.

Then we imagine ourselves sending energy to Briana and to ourselves. When the meditation is over, we talk, sharing our meditation and stories about Glenna. Judy, who is usually less optimistic than I, surprises me by saying that she also meditated and found that Glenna was in a good place. Judy was as surprised as I was.

I don't "believe" in a personal afterlife and thought that "communication with the dead" was just a lot of hokey to make the survivors feel better. But how can I deny my experience? It was so completely the opposite of what I expected. I *felt* the connection between the "living" me and the "dead" Glenna. Our beings are too strong to be encompassed by our bodies. I know that the meditation we did helped Glenna, and I feel as though she has given us a lot of energy too. I feel so close to the women who were at the ritual, even those I don't know. We have shared something very deep, and we wound up actually having a very good time, relaxing and sharing food. A whole new way of working with death, as well as an openness to new possibilities of rebirth, is opening up inside me. I feel deeply moved and awed by our community.

"Last Chance to Chant"

In December 1976, a national conference on Violence Against Women was held in San Francisco. The conference was a landmark in terms of the wide range of women of all ages, classes, races, and backgrounds who participated, as well as in the unification and ongoing action it effected. It was attended by a thousand women and consisted of general sessions and workshops covering thirty areas of violence against women—including rape, child abuse, medical violence, violence against Third World women, women in jails, older women, teenage women, lesbians, violence in religion, psychic action against violence, psychiatric violence, pornography, suicide, and violence between women. Members of the steering committee who were concerned with integrating the spiritual and the political asked Margo Adair, Batya Podos, Starhawk, and me to create a collective ritual to close the conference.

This ritual is a clear example of using a variety of personal and collective meditation techniques for individual and collective change. The four of us who created this ritual came from different backgrounds. None of us had ever worked together before. We employed Womanspirit tools— such as centering, exchanging energy through a circle of hands, bodywork, and meditation—at each meeting, so that we could leave behind our differences and work as one unit.

We had to make a tight structure, as exactly twenty minutes had been alloted for the ritual. Each of us wrote words to be chanted by ourselves or one another. Batya made a three-foot-long sword from cardboard, costume jewelry, and gold paint, "to make it as seductive as possible." As we planned the ritual, we recognized the psychic power of a thousand women spending a weekend focusing on violence and ways to deal with it. We knew that it would be an emotionally charged situation that could go many ways. In the past, we women have often turned anger against ourselves, our children, and one another, or in random outbursts against the patriarchy.

We felt that it was essential to transform the violence we were dealing with and to direct our anger in a focused, ritualistic way. In addition, we all had had the experience of leaving an intense conference diffused and exhausted. We wanted people to leave this one energized and clear. We also wanted to create an experience that would emphasize the connection between the conference and our everyday lives.

The last general session of the conference took place in the basement of Grace Cathedral. As each workshop gave its report, a feeling of the unity of the conference grew. When the reports were over, we began the ritual. Lights, microphones, and video equipment surrounded us—not our usual ritual tools.

As you read this, imagine yourself in a hall with hundreds of women, having spent a painful, intense, and enlightening weekend with personal and collective experiences of violence against women and ways of counteracting it. Imagine yourself living through the ritual. Go through the chants and meditations yourself. Feel the power pouring through you:

HALLIE: "If the idea of a ritual turns you off because it sounds like church, give this one a chance. It's women doing it this time. We've raised a lot of energy this weekend. Anger is an important emotion, and this is not a ritual—like many patriarchal rituals—to disperse our anger. This is a ritual to channel it, on a psychic level, into the kinds of actions we've been talking about this weekend. Rather than letting our anger paralyze us with its intensity or turning it against ourselves and one another, we can use this anger to build a world without violence.

"We'd like everyone to stand as close together as possible in concentric semicircles around the stage, so we can touch one another and keep a continuous stream of energy throughout the room.

"This ritual is a transition from an intense weekend back into our everyday lives. It is an opportunity to psychically transmute the energy and feed ourselves with it, to fight violence and to create peace, to nurture ourselves and one another. What is important is that we trust ourselves, our power, and our wisdom in dealing with that power.

"We will first raise our energy and then direct it towards a sword, the universal symbol of violence. We will then break the sword to release the energy. This act will transform the violence to whatever form each of us chooses. Finally, we will collectively create a vision of a world created by the power we have raised, celebrating our strength. Only take part in whatever feels comfortable to you.

"Spend a few minutes centering by focusing on your breathing. Feel your feet on the ground and your connection with the earth."

STARHAWK: "I will read the lines of this chant and listen for your echo. [As Starhawk reads each phrase the voices answer.] We are sisters! We are mothers! We are lovers! We are workers! We are teachers! We are healers!

At first, the energy in the room is hesitant. Most of the people have never taken part in a feminist ritual. Gradually, the momentum builds, until there is a strong sense of unity in diversity as hundreds of women call out Starhawk's words:

"We have been hungry; we have been overfed; we are old and weary; we are young and anxious; we are ill and in pain; we are well and strong; we are black, brown, white; we speak different languages; we understand without words.

"We have been separated; but we are sisters. We have been murdered and raped—but we are mothers. We have known hatred—but we are lovers. We have felt destruction—but we are workers. We have been kept in ignorance—but we are teachers. We have known violence—but we are healers. We are women; together we are strong.

"We have the power to end violence. We have the courage to love. We have the strength to bring life into the world."

STARHAWK (alone): "We form into circles—small circles—small wombs. Together—reach out, and place your hands on your sister's wombs and feel the life-source. Source, not just of children, but of all creation, all transformation, all change! Feel the power that brings life into being.

"Breathe together and become one. Breathe together and let out our pain. Breathe together, and feel our suffering. Breathe in . . . and out. Breathe in . . . and out. Breathe in . . . and out."

Soon all the women in this huge hall are breathing together. Two women come out of the crowd and pick up the broom from which the sword is hanging. It dangles above our heads, revolving slowly, light glinting off the jewels.

BATYA: "The symbol of the sword is a symbol of rape, violence, war. The symbol of the sword is a symbol of those who conquer, those who have power over, those who own and imprison. . . . Let this sword represent the rapers and destroyers, those who oppress us and do us violence. Let us focus our energy on this sword as their symbol. Let this sword be filled with our anger and rage. Let our anger and rage fill the sword, and, as it is broken, let the patriarchy it represents be broken with it."

HALLIE (gesturing): "Step forward three times, and each time you step forward, throw out your arms as if to throw your anger and rage into the sword. When the sword is broken, feel your own energy—transformed now—coming back into you."

For several long minutes, hundreds of women roar their anger towards the sword. The hall is filled with stomping, shouting, screaming, and crying. Later we find out that a church service was going on above us. The sword turns. A woman steps forward from the circle, seizes the sword and breaks it across her knee, throwing it on the ground. The women cheer and applaud. A small girl and boy pick up the remnants and start to play with them.

HALLIE: "Feel that energy coming back into you, feel it flowing back through your blood and your bones, through

every cell of your body. . . . Feel its wholeness and creativity coursing through you, yours to use however you
want. . . . Let it free you of whatever you want to let go of;
let it fill you with whatever you need. . . . Feel what it is
you let go of . . . and what you absorb."

Rustling. Sighing. Everything looks more vivid and people
somehow more alive.

MARGO: "Now you have transmuted that energy. Now your
energy is free, clear. Close your eyes and with this clarity,
look, feel within yourself, feel the power, the mobilizing
power of your love and angry energy. . . . If you come
across remnants of restricting energy, imagine it dissolv-
ing into the earth through the arches of your feet. . . . Feel
your clarity. You are in contact with the deepest portions
of your being. Your wisdom gives you a vision of a time
that inspires all your creativity—all of our creativity— of a
time without violence— of this vision being brought down
into the present. This vision is right here, right now. Our
action creates a community of strength, of support, of
creativity. Feel our energy resonating together. . . . Feel
ourselves living in harmony with the earth. Feel how that
is, feeling the power of our action to create a time without
violence. Our community is strong, protective, creative,
inspiring—and it exists within the larger community. Our
energy, our actions shall transform that community and
our community shall affect the community it is within.
Feel this energy rippling, encompassing the entire planet
with strength, support, creativity, and harmony. . . . As we
focus on this vision, our resonating energy becomes a
channel for change. . . . Feel our energy resonating together; feel our power. When we leave here today and
move out into the world, our energy, our actions shall
uproot and dissolve all violence. Know how this is so—
feel what you will do to uproot violence. Violence shall be
turned under into the ground of society where it will

decompose and fertilize society to foster new growth. . . .
Our vision grows. Our vision is real and shall be material-
ized. . . . Feel its reality, right here, right now."

The energy in the hall is immense. We are awed by our
power, which feels stronger for the silence.

HALLIE: "Place your hands on the bellies of the women on
either side of you. Feel the energy passing around,
through your hands, your bodies. . . . Gradually let your
breath become sound—energy to live in this world while
creating the new."

Slowly, each of us begins to sound, growing into a voice
that is at once deep and rooted and high and clear. The
power in seven hundred women's voices—united in struggle, passing through violence and vision—rises, cre-
scendoes, is quiet . . .

HALLIE: "We are women, come together from our different
homes, communities, races, classes, sexualities, and liveli-
hoods. We come together to share our strength and wisdom to free ourselves and the world from violence. Now
we have transformed negative energy."

Again, hundreds of voices respond with our new litany:

"We know violence; we end violence. . . . We feel pain; we
heal. . . . We acknowledge suffering; we bring change. . . .
We are women. Together we are strong. Together we are
sisters. Together we are lovers. Together we are workers.
Together we are teachers. Together we are healers."

HALLIE: "Feel how you will walk out of this place. . . . Feel
how you will be as you walk down the streets. . . . Feel how
you will act and think differently in the weeks and months
to come as a result of our being together. Feel how your
life is changed.

"The circle is open but unbroken. The circle continues
in our hearts. The circle continues in our minds. The cir-

cle continues in our bodies. The circle continues in our lives. We are the circle of life."

The Age of Woman

Many historians and spiritual teachers have described this era as "the Age of Woman." The world needs and wants our wisdom and power to help regain the balance so badly needed in human relationships, in the environment, and in our own inner selves. Your future and the future of the world are in your hands. What kind of a world would you like to live in? How can you use or adapt the tools and perspectives in this book to create the world you want? How can you work with others to accomplish this?

Remember that as women we are strong. We create the world. The power of creation and transformation of all is within us. My hope is that this book will be a stepping stone for you along the way, helping you to develop your Womanspirit, to feel the power of the circle of life within yourself, your community, and the planet. Take what is useful and important to you and infuse it with your own spirit. Whatever path you take is ultimately your own. Many others will join you along the way.

About the Author

A pioneer in the feminist spirituality movement, *Hallie Iglehart* publishes extensively and leads Womanspirit groups and workshops throughout the United States and abroad.

A graduate of Brown University, she spent years exploring religious traditions and psychotherapies, especially Jungian theories, Zen Buddhism, and Tibetan Buddhism.

Her increasingly intense studies took her to England, across Europe, and finally to Nepal. She lived in India for a time and met with numerous Tibetan refugees. In the shadow of the Himalayas, she found much of her classical Western education and "programming" receding as she discovered a religious tradition that allowed for more equality of the sexes; embraced compassion as a concrete mandate, rather than an abstract theory; celebrated timeless rituals that still have the power to touch the inner person and heighten spiritual awareness; looked to nature as the paramount teacher; and made possible a rich integration of the spiritual and the everyday in the lives of its adherents.

From this encounter, Iglehart sensed the first part of an ongoing spiritual awakening. She became acutely aware that a new path of feminist, postpatriarchal spirituality had to be charted for herself, and for women and sympathetic men everywhere.

During this watershed time, many of her developing ideas came into sharpened focus. She realized that Buddhism, despite its intriguing possibilities, for many reasons (not the least, an understated but pervasive sexism) held no final answers.

Returning to the United States, she moved to San Francisco and continued her studies in meditation, yoga, and healing, and became involved in the women's health movement. Then she began teaching classes in feminist spirituality, stressing the essence of religion as facilitating energy-sharing; the failure of established religions to address female spiritual questions and needs; and the importance—for men as well as women—of discovering one's internal power and learning to trust the inner self, which is the surest guide along the spiritual path.

While working and teaching, Iglehart became a regular contributor to the newly founded *WomanSpirit* magazine, sharing her insights on synthesizing the feminist and spiritual movements. She also began the research and reflection which culminated in the present book.

She makes her home in the San Francisco Bay Area.